Vorwort zur zweiten Auflage

Es ist sehr erfreulich, wie das Berliner Schloss, das kurz vor seiner baulichen Fertigstellung steht, wieder wie selbstverständlich seine Rolle als zentrales Gebäude der Stadt wieder aufnimmt. Es hatte städtebaulich die Funktion der Kathedrale in den französischen Städten: Es markierte seit Jahrhunderten die Stadtmitte und trug wesentlich zu der überaus reichen aber auch umstrittenen Geschichte Berlins bei. Es füllte nach seiner Sprengung weiter zahlreiche repräsentative Bücher – aber auch diese waren noch nicht vollkommen, fehlte ihnen allen doch die jüngere, die Wiederaufbaugeschichte.

Ein kleines Buch über ein großes Werk so kompetent zu gestalten, grenzt für mich schon fast an ein Wunder. Vielen Dank für den Mut dazu! Es will kein wissenschaftliches Werk sein, sondern den Leser mit geringen Kenntnissen über das Berliner Schloss so umfassend informieren, dass jeder versteht, warum dieses vor nun schon 68 Jahren gesprengte Zentralgebäude Berlins zurückkehren musste. Das neue Schloss von Berlin wird das erste sein, das die Bürger Deutschlands freiwillig bezahlten – und das nicht auf Befehl von oben gebaut wurde: Weil es zurückersehnt wurde!

Berlin, den 3. Januar 2018
Wilhelm von Boddien

Foreword to the second edition

It is very gratifying to see how the Berlin Palace, shortly before its completion, is quite naturally resuming its role as the city's main building. As an urban landmark, it had the same function as a cathedral in French cities: for centuries it highlighted the city centre and made a major contribution to the exceedingly rich, albeit controversial, history of Berlin. After it was demolished, it continued to be the subject of many prestigious books – but none of these were complete, as none of them included the most recent part of the palace's history, the story of its reconstruction.

I find it quite incredible that such a little book can provide so much competent information about such a great work, and I would like to thank the author for having the courage to take on this task. The book does not purport to be scientific or academic, its aim is to provide wide background information to readers with little previous knowledge about the Berlin Palace, so that everyone can understand why it was essential for this key building, blown up 68 years ago, to return to Berlin. The new Berlin Palace will be the first one that German citizens have paid for voluntarily – and which was not built on orders from above, but because the population longed for its return.

Berlin, 3rd January 2018
Wilhelm von Boddien

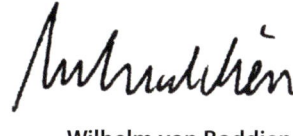

Wilhelm von Boddien

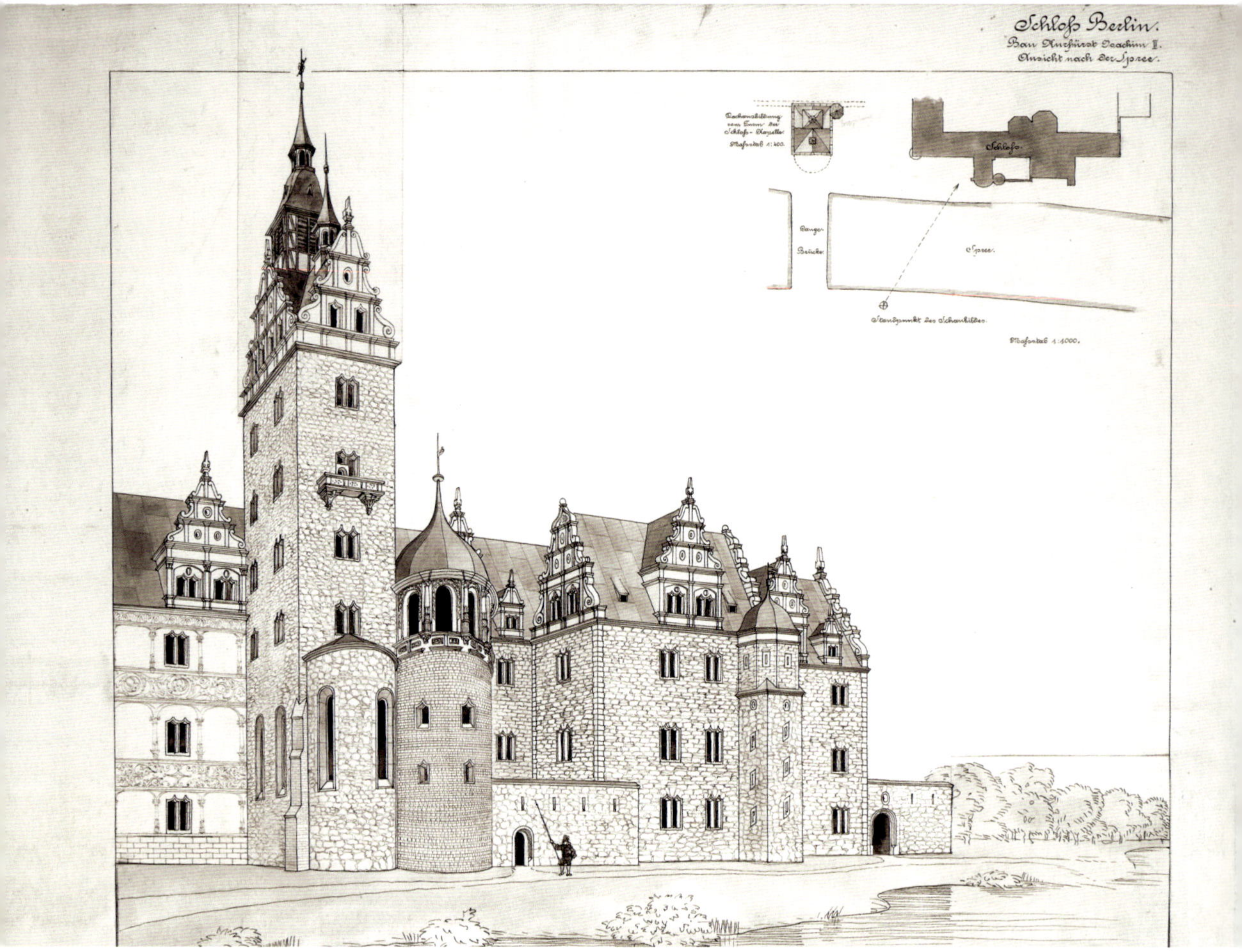

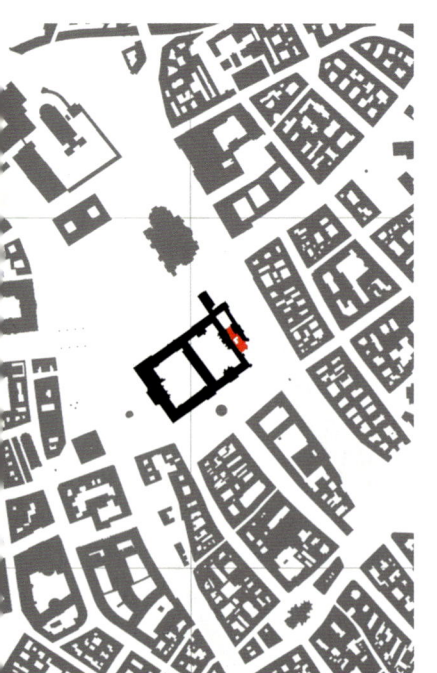

Rekonstruktionsversuch von Albert Geyer. Es existieren keinerlei Abbildungen der Burg. | Attempt to reconstruct the castle by Albert Geyer. No pictures of the castle exist.

Zustand Schloss um 1450 | Outline of the castle around 1450

Die Burg

Berlin erscheint erst spät auf der europäischen Landkarte. 1237 gegründet, hatten zu diesem Zeitpunkt London und Paris ein schon mehr als tausendjähriges Alter erreicht. Eine ernstzunehmende Größe wurde die Stadt an der Spree erst 1443 mit dem Bau der Hohenzollernburg an der Schnittstelle der beiden mittelalterlichen Gründungen Berlin und Cölln. Dabei war die Burganlage zunächst alles andere als gewollt: 1448 setzten die Berliner Patrizier den Bauplatz Kurfürst Friedrichs II. unter Wasser, um den Weiterbau zu verhindern. Ein glückloses Unterfangen, das als „Berliner Unwille" in die Geschichte einging.

The castle

Berlin did not find its way onto the map of Europe until quite late. When the city was founded in 1237, London and Paris had already been around for more than a thousand years. In fact, the town on the river Spree was not really taken seriously until Hohenzollern ruler, Frederick II, decided to build a castle at the convergence of the two medieval settlements, Berlin and Cölln, in 1443. The castle complex was anything but popular: In 1448, Berlin's patricians flooded the construction site in an attempt to prevent further work on the project. Although unsuccessful, this act of protest went down in history as the "Berliner Unwille" (Berlin's disapproval).

MARC **METZGER**

DAS BERLINER
SCHLOSS
THE BERLIN PALACE

BERLIN STORY VERLAG

Bildnachweis

Inhalt

Impressum

Metzger, Marc:
Das Berliner Schloss
2., aktualisierte Auflage —
 Berlin: Berlin Story Verlag 2018
ISBN 978-3-95723-101-7

© Berlin Story Verlag GmbH
Leuschnerdamm 7, 10999 Berlin
Tel.: (030) 20 91 17 80
Fax: (030) 69 20 40 059

UStID: DE291153827
AG Berlin (Charlottenburg)
 HRB 152956 B
www.BerlinStory-Verlag.de
E-Mail: Service@BerlinStory-Verlag.de

Translation: Pamela Hirsinger
Satz und Layout: Norman Bösch

Printed by **LASER**LINE

WWW.BERLINSTORY.DE

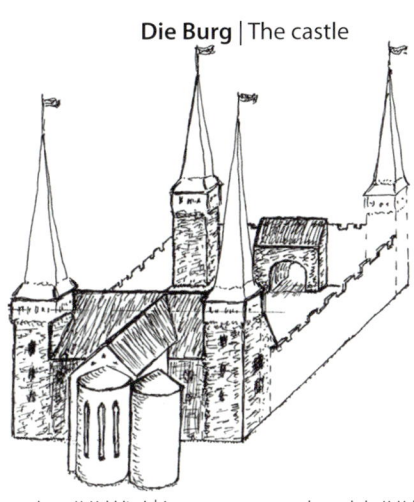

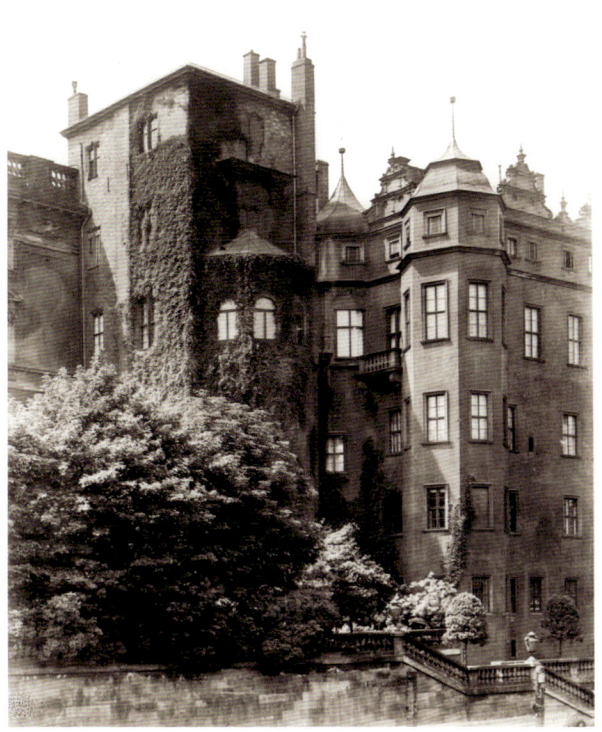

Erasmuskapelle und Grüner Hut | Erasmus Chapel and "Green Hat"

Rekonstruktionsversuch von H. Vahldieck | Attempt to reconstruct the castle by H. Vahldieck

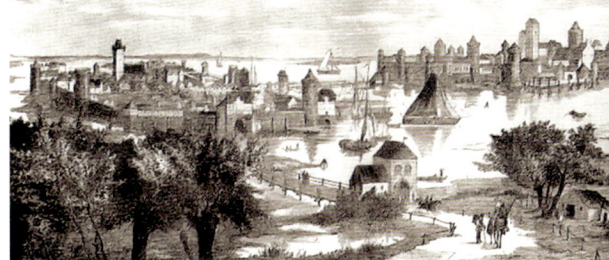

Berlin und Cölln um 1250 | Berlin and Cölln around 1250

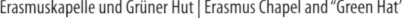

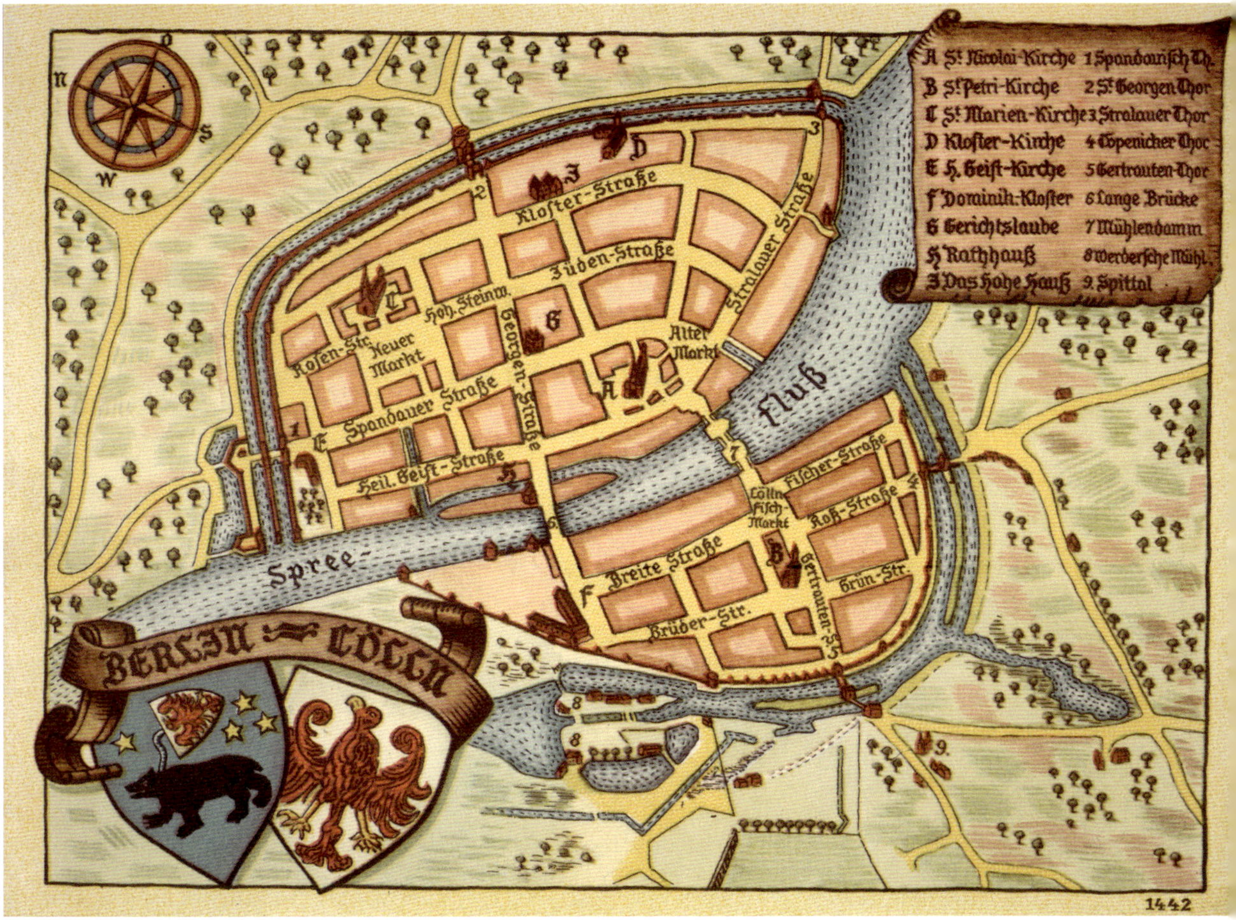
A St. Nicolai-Kirche
B St. Petri-Kirche
C St. Marien-Kirche
D Kloster-Kirche
E H. Geist-Kirche
F Dominik-Kloster
G Gerichtslaube
H Rathhauß
J Das hohe Hauß
1 Spandauisch Th.
2 St. Georgen Thor
3 Stralauer Thor
4 Copenicker Thor
5 Gertrauten-Thor
6 Lange Brücke
7 Mühlendamm
8 Werdersche Mühl.
9. Spittal
Kloster-Straße
Juden-Straße
Stralauer Straße
Hoh. Steinw.
Georgen-Straße
Rosen-Str.
Neuer Markt
Alter Markt
Spandauer Straße
Heil. Geist-Straße
Fluß
Spree
Fischer-Straße
Roß-Straße
Cölln Fisch-Markt
Breite Straße
Brüder-Str.
Gertrauten-Str.
Brüder-Str.
1442

Nachträglich angefertigte Karte von Berlin und Cölln um 1442 | Map of Berlin and Cölln around 1442

Das Schloss Joachims II. in der Südansicht, 1690 | The palace of Joachim II, south view

Zustand Schloss 1688 | Outline of the palace

Das Renaissanceschloss

Kurfürst Joachim II. baute um 1540 die spätmittelalterliche Burg zu einem Renaissanceschloss aus. Sein Architekt Konrad Krebs schuf eine L-förmige Anlage mit zwei markanten Eckerkern auf der Südseite.

1647, kurz vor Ende des Dreißigjährigen Kriegs, war es der Große Kurfürst Friedrich Wilhelm, der eine Allee vom Schloss ausgehend in westlicher Richtung anlegen ließ, die ihm als Reitweg dienen sollte. Noch immer war das Schloss am Rande der Stadt situiert – und niemand hätte damals geahnt, dass aus jenem Reitweg eines Tages die pulsierende Straße Unter den Linden erwachsen würde.

The Renaissance Palace

Around 1540, Elector Joachim II began to transform the late medieval castle into a Renaissance-style palace. His architect, Konrad Krebs, created an L-shaped building with two distinctive corner oriels on the south side.

In 1647, shortly before the end of the Thirty Years' War, Great Elector Frederick William ordered that an avenue should be created – starting at the palace and running in a westerly direction – for use as a bridle road. At that time, the palace was still located on the outskirts of the town – who at that time would have thought that this bridle road would someday become the lively *Unter den Linden* boulevard!

Dominikanerkloster (Mitte) und Schloss (rechts) von der Langen Brücke aus, vor 1700 | Dominican monastery and palace (r.) seen from Lange Brücke

Der Lynartrakt | Lynar wing

Schlossplatz um 1690 | Palace Square around 1690

Berlin und Cölln um 1652, im Vordergrund die Lindenallee | Berlin and Cölln around 1652, in the foreground the avenue of lime trees

Idealentwurf Andreas Schlüters für den Barockumbau des Schlosses, Südansicht, 1704 | Andreas Schlüter's design for a baroque transformation, south view

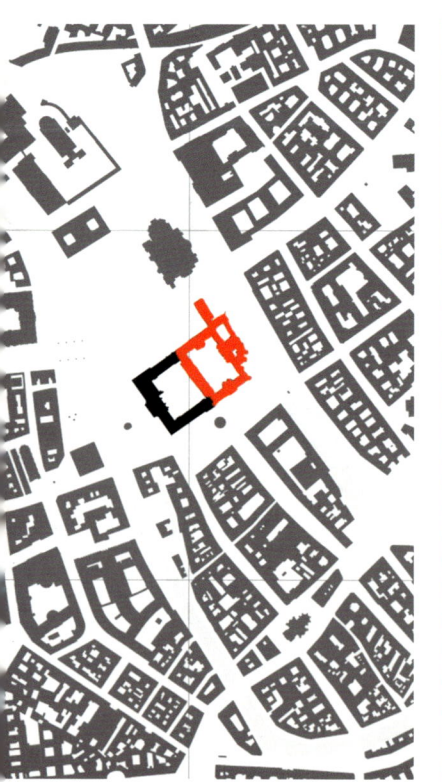

Zustand Schloss 1706 | Outline of the palace

Das Barockschloss

Das Berliner Schloss in einen Bau von Weltrang zu verwandeln, schickte sich Kurfürst Friedrich III. an, der sich 1701 selbst zum König in Preußen krönte. Als er im Mai desselben Jahres mit seiner Entourage in seinen umgestalteten Palazzo einritt, hatte Andreas Schlüter, sein zum Baumeister beförderter Bildhauer aus Danzig, den geplanten Barockumbau noch nicht vollendet. Doch wusste Schlüter zu glänzen: Das Hauptportal mit den mächtigen, bislang in dieser Form ungekannten Kolossalsäulen stellte selbst sein Versailler Pendant in den Schatten. Der Hof, dessen Skulpturen die griechische Mythologie aufgreifen, mit seiner dahinter angesiedelten Gigantentreppe gilt als Meisterschöpfung Schlüters.

The Baroque Palace

Elector Frederick III, who crowned himself King in Prussia in 1701, set about transforming the Berlin Palace into a building of worldwide renown. When Frederick and his entourage rode into the redesigned palazzo in May of the same year, Andreas Schlüter, a sculptor from Danzig who had been promoted to court architect, had not yet completed his baroque transformation. His work nevertheless made a stunning impression: The main portal with its colossal columns, unknown in this form up to that time, even outshone its counterpart in Versailles. The courtyard with its sculptures portraying scenes of Greek mythology and the Giant Staircase behind it is considered to be Schlüter's greatest masterpiece.

Nordansicht mit Portal V | North façade with Portal V

Deckengemälde | Ceiling painting, Schwarze Adlerkammer

Schlüterhof, um 1740 | Schlüter Courtyard around 1740

Eduard Gärtners berühmtes Schlüterhof-Gemälde, um 1850 | Eduard Gärtner's famous Schlüter Courtyard painting

Kurfürstenbrücke (Lange Brücke) und Schloss | Kurfürsten bridge (Lange Brücke) and palace

Eckvoute des Rittersaals | Corner haunch of Knights' Hall

Darstellung von Goerd Peschken, die die Fernwirkung des Münzturms von der Straße Unter den Linden aus illustriert |
Drawing by Goerd Peschken showing the envisaged Mint Tower from Unter den Linden

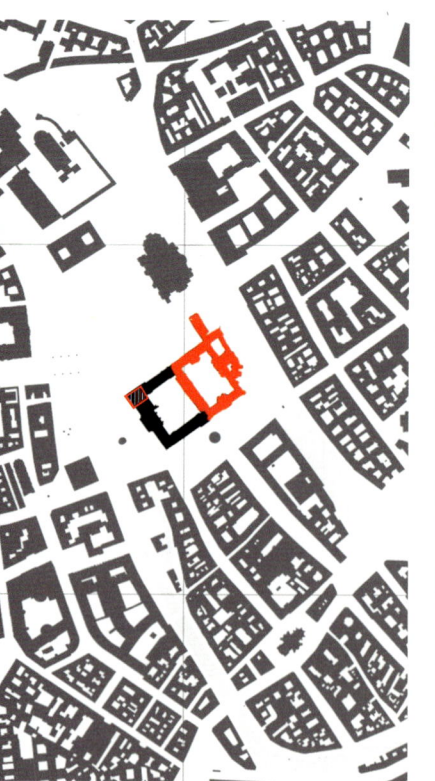

Zustand Schloss 1706 mit Münzturm |
Outline of the palace, with the Mint Tower

Die Münzturm-katastrophe

Schlüters Ruhm währte nicht lange. An der nordwestlichen Ecke des Areals hatte der König einen von weit her sichtbaren Münzturm gefordert. Schlüter gründete diesen auf einer nicht tragfähigen Torflinse. Es kam zum Grundbruch: Der Turm neigte sich und musste aufwendig rückgebaut werden. Schlüter verlor seine Stellung als Baumeister, war fortan in der Hauptsache Hofbildhauer und emigrierte 1713 nach St. Petersburg, wo er im Jahr darauf verstarb.

In der Ufa-Verfilmung *Andreas Schlüter* von 1942, die den Einsturz des Münzturms zum Thema hat, mimt Heinrich George den genialischen Künstler, der an der Münzturmkatastrophe scheitert.

The Mint Tower disaster

Schlüter's fame was short lived. The king had ordered him to build a Mint Tower that would be visible far and wide at the north-west corner of the site. Unfortunately, the ground Schlüter chose to build this on was an instable peat lens. When the ground gave way, the tower started to lean and had to be demolished at great expense. Schlüter lost his job as court architect but continued to work as court sculptor before emigrating to St. Petersburg in 1713, where he died a year later.

In the 1942 Ufa movie *Andreas Schlüter*, which has the collapse of the Mint Tower as its theme, Heinrich George played the role of the brilliant artist whose downfall had been the Mint Tower disaster.

Filmszene aus „Andreas Schlüter": Der Bau des Münzturms | Scene from the film "Andreas Schlüter": construction of the Mint Tower

Entwurf des Münzturms, 1706 | Draft of the Mint Tower

Friedrich I. prüft Schlüters Pläne | Frederick I reviewing Schlüter's plans

Heinrich George als Andreas Schlüter | Heinrich George as Andreas Schlüter

Portal V, IV und die Eosanderschulter an der Lustgartenseite, um 1750 | Portals V, IV and the Eosander risalit facing the Lustgarten, around 1750

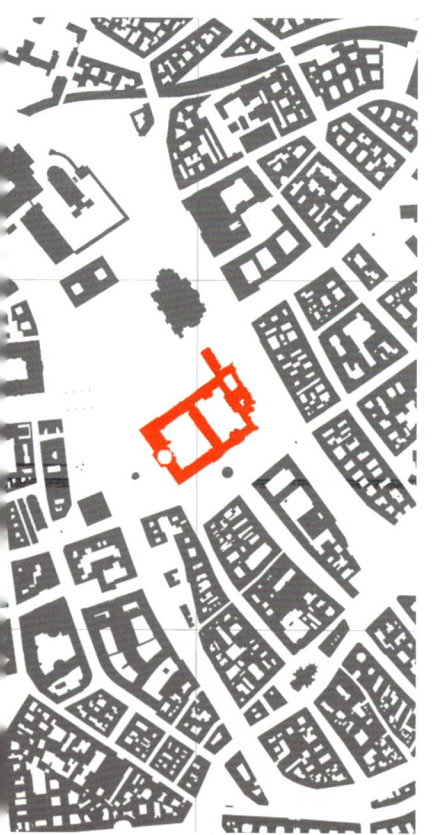

Zustand Schloss 1716 | Outline of the palace

Erweiterung durch Eosander

Nach Schlüters Entlassung beauftragte der König Johann Eosander gen. von Göthe 1706 als dessen Nachfolger. Dieser verdoppelte den Bau in seiner Grundfläche, indem er nach Westen einen zweiten Hof hinzufügte. Von nun an reichte das Schloss vom Ostufer der Spreeinsel bis zu ihrem westlichen Rand. Doch Eosander erlitt ein ähnliches Schicksal wie Schlüter vor ihm. Als Friedrich I. 1713 verstarb, entließ ihn dessen als sparsam geltender Sohn, Friedrich Wilhelm I., und entschied, nach zweijährigem Baustillstand, dass Martin Böhme den Großen Schlosshof nach Süden hin im Zuge einer Notmaßnahme schließen solle. Die weiteren Vorhaben Eosanders, etwa die Errichtung eines Turms auf dem Portal an der Westseite, wurden nicht mehr aufgegriffen.

Extension by Eosander

After dismissing Schlüter, the king appointed Johann Eosander von Göthe as Schlüter's successor in 1706. Eosander doubled the base area of the building by adding a second courtyard to the west. Now the palace extended right from the east bank to the west bank of the Spree island. Eosander, however, suffered a fate similar to that of his predecessor. When Frederick I died in 1713, his son and heir, Frederick William I, who had a reputation for austerity, dismissed Eosander and after a two-year interruption in the construction work decided that Martin Böhme should close the south side of the Great Palace Courtyard as an emergency measure. Eosander's other planned building projects, for example the construction of a tower on the west portal, were never realised, either.

Eosanders Portal III | Eosander's Portal III

Der Große Schlosshof nach Süden | Grand Courtyard, looking to the south

Eosanders geplanter Turm auf Portal III | Planned tower on Portal III

Die von Martin Böhme vollendete Südseite mit den Portalen II und I | South façade completed by Martin Böhme, showing Portals II and I

Schlossbrücke, Schloss und Schlossfreiheit um 1855 | Palace Bridge, palace and patricians' houses (Schlossfreiheit) around 1855

Zustand Schloss 1853 | Outline of the palace

Die Kuppel

Hofbaumeister Karl Friedrich Schinkel nahm sich des Schlosses an, nachdem er in dessen Umfeld bereits eine Reihe eigener Bauten fertig gestellt hatte. Angeregt durch den Kronprinzen plante er, Eosanders ungekröntes Triumphbogenportal an der Westseite mit nunmehr hundertjähriger Verzögerung um eine Kuppel zu ergänzen. Jedoch vermochte er nicht, seinen Entwurf zu Lebzeiten umzusetzen. Erst sein Schüler August Stüler verlieh Portal III bis 1853 jenen fortan als Kapelle genutzten Abschluss.

An die fünfzig Jahre später erweiterte Julius Raschdorff die Stadtsilhouette ein weiteres Mal: Mit seinem Berliner Dom schuf er in Zusammenspiel mit dem Schloss ein Konzert der Kuppeln am Ende der Linden, das jahrzehntelang als Postkartenpanorama stellvertretend für Berlin stehen sollte.

The dome

Court architect Karl Friedrich Schinkel started to take an interest in the palace after designing and completing a number of other buildings in the immediate vicinity. Spurred on by the crown prince, he committed himself to building a dome to crown Eosander's triumphal arch on the west side of the palace – 100 years later than originally planned. Although Schinkel was unable to make his design a reality within his own lifetime, his pupil August Stüler completed Portal III in 1853 by adding this final element, which from then on was used as a chapel.

Some fifty years later, Julius Raschdorff extended the city skyline once more: The dome of his Berlin Cathedral, together with that of the neighbouring palace, formed an architectural duo that became the symbol of Berlin on panorama postcards for decades.

Schlosskapelle | Palace chapel

Das Zusammenspiel von Dom- und Schlosskuppel, um 1937 | Cathedral and palace dome ensemble around 1937

Luftaufnahme um 1920, am Horizont die auf Portal V zulaufende Straße Unter den Linden | Aerial photograph around 1920, showing Unter den Linden to the right

Dom und Schloss zur Kaiserzeit | Cathedral and palace during the Imperial era

Die in der Renaissance überformte und ausgebaute Burganlage an der Spree | Castle complex, as modified and extended during the Renaissance

Das Schloss im Gefüge der Stadt

König Friedrich I. hatte die über Jahrhunderte gewachsene Wasserseite, die er einst ebenfalls barock gestalten wollte, aus Geldnot beibehalten und damit das Gegenstück zur altstädtischen Situation jenseits der Spree bewahrt. Der Grüne Hut, ein Wehrturm der ehemaligen Stadtmauer Cöllns, blieb als ältester Bauteil des Schlosses bis zuletzt erhalten. Das Schlossgärtchen an der Spree bildete eine Ruheoase inmitten der Stadt.

The palace as an integral part of the city

King Frederick I had intended to give the waterfront façade, evolved historically over centuries, a baroque appearance, too, but had to leave it unchanged due to lack of funds. Thus it was preserved as a counterpart to the "old town" on the other side of the Spree. The Green Hat (Grüner Hut) – a fortified tower of the former town walls of Cölln, as the oldest part of the palace, survived right up to the palace's demolition.

Schlossgärtchen, 1901 | The palace garden

Die der ehemaligen Stadt Cölln zugewandte Südfassade markierte mit Portal II den Schlusspunkt der Breiten Straße. Ergänzt wurde diese Sichtachse durch den Neptunbrunnen, der 1891 auf dem Schlossplatz installiert wurde. Er, ein Geschenk des Berliner Magistrats an den Kaiser, geschaffen von Reinhold Begas, gab dem Platz fortan die Mitte.

Breite Strasse ended at Portal II, which was part of the south façade, facing the former town of Cölln. The Neptune Fountain installed on Palace Square in 1891 completed this vista. The fountain, created by Reinhold Begas, was a present from the Berlin city council to the Emperor and from then on adorned the centre of the square.

Neptunbrunnen vor Portal II | Neptune Fountain in front of Portal II

Portal II als Schlusspunkt der Breiten Straße | Portal II at the end of Breite Strasse

Der Schlossplatz von Westen | Palace Square viewed from the west

Lustgartenseite des Schlosses, im Vordergrund die Amazonenskulptur vor dem Alten Museum, um 1869 |
Palace façade facing the Lustgarten, in the foreground "Amazon on horseback" statue (Old Museum)

Die Skulpturen zweier Rosse-bändiger aus St. Petersburg, aufgestellt vor Portal IV, waren ein Geschenk des Zaren Nikolaus I. an seinen Schwager Friedrich Wilhelm IV. Ab 1861 schmückte außerdem eine aus Amazone und Löwenkämpfer bestehende Figurengruppe die Treppe zu Schinkels Altem Museum. Sie traten seither über den Lustgarten hinweg in Kommunikation mit den gegenüberliegenden Rosse-bändigern und verliehen dem Platz dadurch seine Rahmung.

The famous sculptures, the St. Petersburg "Horse Tamers", installed in front of Portal IV, were a present from Tsar Nicholas I to his brother-in-law, Frederick William IV. A few years later, in 1861, two bronze statues "Amazon on horseback" and "The lion fighter" were installed at the sides of the steps leading up to Schinkel's Old Museum (Altes Museum). For many years, these two statues and the horse tamers stood in architectural dialogue across the Lustgarten, beautifully framing the square.

Die Rossebändiger vor Portal IV, 1933 | "Horse Tamer" statues in front of Portal IV

Schlossfreiheit um 1892 | Patrician town houses around 1892

Nationaldenkmal mit dem Reiterstandbild Wilhelms I. | National Monument with equestrian statue of William I

Die von Eosander als Schauseite konzipierte Westfassade verlangte geradezu nach einem adäquaten städtebaulichen Gegengewicht, das die Wuchtigkeit seines Triumphbogenportals auffangen würde. In Form des Nationaldenkmals wurde dies 1897, nach dem Abriss die Sicht versperrender Bürgerhäuser an der Schlossfreiheit, Realität. Das Denkmal erinnerte an die Reichsgründung 1871 und zeigte Wilhelm I. zu Pferde, umgeben von einer Löwengruppe und einem Kolonnadengang.

The west façade, which Eosander had designed as the palace's "showcase" façade, virtually cried out for a suitable building to uphold the city's architectural integrity and counterbalance the massive triumphal arch. In 1897, following the demolition of several patrician town houses which were blocking the view, the National Monument was built to create this counterpart. The monument commemorated the foundation of the German Reich in 1871 and consisted of an equestrian statue of William I surrounded by a group of lions and a colonnade.

Schloss und Nationaldenkmal, um 1895 | Palace and National Monument around 1895

Die Innengestaltung

Im Paradegeschoss, dem zweiten Obergeschoss des Schlosses, den Kleinen Schlosshof einrahmend und wie auf einer Perlenschnur aufgereiht, befanden sich die einst von Schlüter geschaffenen Raumfolgen. In ihrer Mitte, in direkter Folge der Gigantentreppe, der Schweizersaal – benannt nach der Schweizergarde, die hier Einlass gewährte und die Eingänge zu den Paradekammern bewachte. Der Rittersaal, der Thronsaal, von dem aus die Monarchen zum Volke sprachen, orientierte sich in Richtung Lustgarten. Eosanders anschließende Bildergalerie überführte in den Weißen Saal, der zuletzt von Ernst von Ihne aufwendig aus- und umgebaut wurde. Er, als letztes maßgebliches Attribut der Innengestaltung, war Schauplatz zahlreicher festlicher Veranstaltungen der Kaiserzeit.

Interior design

The so-called "parade chambers", designed by Schlüter, on the second floor of the palace, were arranged like a string of beads around the small courtyard. In the centre, directly above the Giant Staircase, was the Swiss Hall – named after the Swiss Guard which guarded the entrance to the parade chambers. The Knights' Hall, which was also the throne room, looked out onto the Lustgarten and was the room from where the monarchs addressed their people. Adjacent to the Knights' Hall was Eosander's picture gallery, which in turn led into the White Hall, last elaborately renovated and modified by Ernst von Ihne. This hall, as the last significant interior design feature to be added, was the venue of many festive events in the days of the German Empire.

Rittersaal, um 1900 |
Knights' Hall around 1900

Gemäldegalerie, vor 1914 | Picture gallery, before 1914

Der Weiße Saal in der Fassung Ihnes, um 1905 | White Hall, as modified by Ihne, around 1905

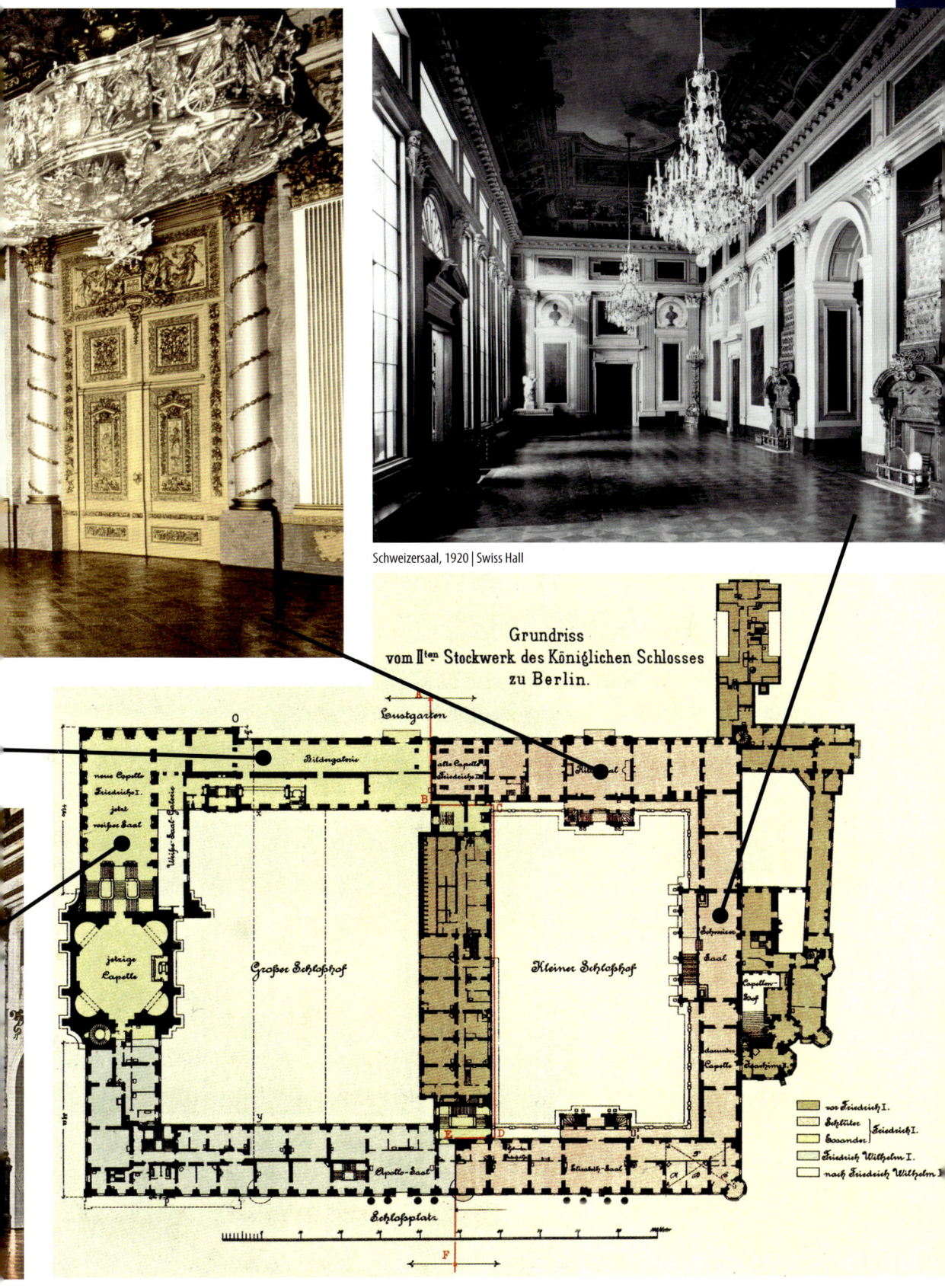

Schweizersaal, 1920 | Swiss Hall

Grundriss
vom II^{ten} Stockwerk des Königlichen Schlosses
zu Berlin.

Alexander von Humboldt, 1843

Die Kunstkammer des Schlosses, 1696 | Palace art chambers

Keimzelle der Museumsinsel

Im 16. Jahrhundert gegründet, im Dreißigjährigen Krieg der Verwahrlosung anheim gefallen, vom Großen Kurfürsten Friedrich Wilhelm wiederbelebt, sorgte die Sammelwut der Kurfürsten und Könige für ein rasantes Anwachsen der Bestände der schlosseigenen Kunst- und Wunderkammern. Bald platzten sie aus allen Nähten. In der Folge wurden mehr und mehr Objekte ausgelagert und von Fachleuten sukzessive zu komplexen Sammlungen weiterentwickelt. Mit Gründung der Universität 1810 realisierte Alexander von Humboldt erstmals auch eine akademische Lehrschau der Wissenschaftssammlungen. 1830 eröffnete Schinkels Altes Museum und machte weitere Objekte der Öffentlichkeit zugänglich. Die kontinuierliche Ausbildung der Museumsinsel, aus dem Schloss heraus erwachsen, war nicht mehr aufzuhalten.

Birth of Museum Island (Museumsinsel)

Founded in the 16th century, neglected and forgotten during the Thirty Years' War and revived by Great Elector Frederick William, the palace's art chambers and curiosity cabinets soon became filled with new works of art and exhibits thanks to the electors' and kings' passion for collecting. It was not long before the rooms were bursting at the seams. As a result, more and more exhibits were stored elsewhere and transformed into complex collections by various experts. After foundation of the Berlin University in 1810, Alexander von Humboldt presented an academic exhibition of the scientific collections for the very first time. Schinkel's Altes Museum was inaugurated in 1830 and made further works and exhibits accessible to the public. The continuous expansion of the Museumsinsel, which had its beginnings in the palace, could no longer be stopped.

Uli-Figur | Uli figure

Gedenkkopf | Memorial head

Schloss und Museumsinsel, um 1920 | Palace and Museum Island around 1920

Ein Ort mit Geschichte

Über Jahrhunderte war das Schloss Schauplatz historischer Ereignisse. Hatten am 18. März 1848 die Bürger auf dem Schlossplatz eine Revolution losgetreten, die in heftige Barrikadenkämpfe in der nahegelegenen Breiten Straße mündete, wurde ein Jahr später der Preußische Landtag, das erste nach einer Verfassung gewählte Parlament in Preußen, im Schloss gegründet.

Im Zuge der Reichsgründung 1871, nach gewonnenem Krieg gegen Frankreich – die Einwohnerzahl steuerte bereits auf eine Million zu – wurde das Schloss, das das Staatszentrum Preußens darstellte, nun zur Mitte des Kaiserreichs. Die Eröffnung des Reichstags 1888 feierte man mit großem Gestus – wo sonst? – im Weißen Saal des Schlosses.

Am 1. August 1914 rief Kaiser Wilhelm II. von Portal V den Krieg aus – ohne zu ahnen, dass es vier Jahre später kein Kaiserreich mehr geben würde. Die Revolution vom November 1918 am Ende des Ersten Weltkriegs zwang ihn schließlich zur Abdankung. Wilhelm ging ins holländische Exil und das Schloss verwaiste daraufhin für zwei Jahre.

A place steeped in history

The Berlin Palace had been the scene of historic events for centuries: On 18th March 1848, for example, the citizens of Berlin triggered off a revolution in Palace Square, resulting in violent street battles in nearby Breite Strasse. Just one year later, the Landtag of Prussia, the first Prussian parliament to be elected on a constitution-

Kämpfe der Märzrevolution 1848 | March Revolution conflicts

al basis, was inaugurated in the palace.

Following foundation of the German Empire in 1871 after victory over France – Berlin's population was rapidly approaching the million mark – the palace which had formed the hub of the Prussian state now became the centre of the German Empire. When the Reichstag was opened in 1888, this event was celebrated with a lot of pomp and glory in – who would have

guessed – the palace's White Hall.

On 1st August 1914, Emperor William II announced general mobilisation from the balcony of Portal V – not knowing that the empire would no longer exist in four years' time. The November 1918 revolution which followed the end of World War I eventually forced him to abdicate. William went into exile in the Netherlands and the palace stood deserted for the next two years.

Eröffnung des Reichstags im Weißen Saal, 1888 | White Hall 1888, ceremonial opening of the Reichstag

Kaiser Wilhelm II. spricht am Anbeginn des Ersten Weltkriegs vom Balkon des Schlosses | Emperor William II addresses the German people from the palace balcony following the outbreak of WWI

Mobilmachung 1914 | General mobilisation

Revolutionstage 1918 | Scenes from the 1918 revolution

Revolutionstage 1918 | Scenes from the 1918 revolution

Zum ersten Mal Museum

Mit dem Ende der Monarchie in Deutschland hatte das Berliner Schloss seine politische Bedeutung eingebüßt. In den Folgejahren erfand es sich völlig neu. 1920 etablierte man erstmals eine Museumsnutzung und öffnete den Bau damit gänzlich der Bevölkerung. Er beherbergte nun ein Schlossmuseum, das den Besuchern Einblicke in die ehemaligen Prachtsäle der Hohenzollern gewährte, auch die Kunstgewerbesammlung wurde hier ausgestellt. Die Liste der neuen Nutzer war lang: Ein Museum für Leibesübungen zog ein, zudem fanden Vereine und private Mieter hier Quartier. Der Schlüterhof fungierte als öffentlicher Konzertort, dessen Akustik bis heute als eine der besten Berlins bekannt ist.

First-time use as a museum

After the end of the German monarchy, the Berlin Palace no longer had any political significance. In the years that followed its purpose was redefined. In 1920, the palace was used as museum for the very first time and the entire building was opened to the public. It now housed a palace museum, giving visitors an insight into the former ceremonial rooms of the Hohenzollern family and showing the arts and crafts collection. The list of new tenants was long: a museum for gymnastics moved in and various societies, associations and private tenants also found a new home in the palace. The Schlüter Courtyard was used as a venue for public concerts and to this very day still has the reputation of having some of the best acoustics in Berlin.

Die Rote Samtkammer mit Schätzen des Kunstgewerbemuseums, 1921 | Treasures from the Museum of Arts and Crafts

Thronzimmer der Königskammern mit Kunstgewerbemuseum, 1921 | Throne room as part of the Museum of Arts and Crafts

Gründamastene Kammer der Königskammern, Museumsraum für Berliner Porzellan, 1921 | The Kings Chambers, display of Berlin porcelain

Museum für Leibesübungen, 1930 | Museum for Physical Education

Das Schloss im Nationalsozialismus

In der Germania-Planung Albert Speers, die einen radikalen Umbau Berlins nach nationalsozialistischer Doktrin vorsah, blieb das Schloss unangetastet. Während östlich der Spree großflächige Abrisse und Straßenverbreiterungen geplant waren, sollte das Ensemble bestehend aus Schloss, Dom, Museumsinsel und Forum Fridericianum dagegen in ein „Freilichtmuseum des Zweiten Reichs" verwandelt werden. Das Schloss fungierte fortan im Lichte monumental inszenierter Aufmärsche als bloße Kulisse für Hakenkreuzfahnen, die den Rahmen für den gegenüberliegenden, erst 1935 gepflasterten und damit zum Paradeplatz umfunktionierten Lustgarten lieferten. Aus der einstigen Gartenoase war unter den Nazis ein kahler, unwirtlicher Platz geworden.

Im Zweiten Weltkrieg blieb das Schloss lange Zeit weitestgehend unzerstört. Erst nach einem verheerenden Bombenangriff am 3. Februar 1945 brannte es mehrere Tage lichterloh.

The palace during the National Socialist era

The Berlin Palace remained totally unaffected by Albert Speer's plans for Germania, involving radical rebuilding of Berlin in line with Nationalist Socialist ideology. While large developed areas to the east of the Spree were to be demolished and streets were to be widened, the architectural ensemble of palace, cathedral, Museum I sland and Forum Fridericianum were to be turned into an "open-air museum of the Second Reich". From now on, the palace merely served as a background for the swastika flags that accompanied the monumental parades staged in the Lustgarten opposite the palace. By 1935, the Nazis had turned the former green oasis into a bleak and inhospitable place by plastering it over and turning it into a parade ground.

The palace remained largely undamaged throughout World War II and it was not until 3rd February 1945 that a devastating air raid set it ablaze for several days.

Berlin im Olympiafieber, 1936 | Berlin in Olympic fever

Heldengedenktag, März 1935 | Memorial Day, March 1935

Luthertag, November 1933 | Reformation Day

Kundgebung anläßlich der Olympischen Sommerspiele, 1936 | Rally during the 1936 Olympic Games

Die Ruine des Schlosses, 1945 | The palace in ruins

Die Ruine

Fünf Jahre lang prägte die Schlossruine die Berliner Mitte. Doch nicht nur die Außenmauern hatten dem Bombardement im Wesentlichen standgehalten, auch existierten noch nutzbare Räumlichkeiten. Die Berliner, in Folge von NS-Diktatur und Krieg kulturell ausgehungert, konnten 1946 im Weißen Saal eine Schau französischer Impressionisten erleben, nachdem bereits zuvor in der Präsentation *Berlin plant* der angedachte Wiederaufbau der Stadt thematisiert worden war. 1948 glorifizierte eine letzte Ausstellung im Schloss das hundertjährige Jubiläum der Revolution. Und auch sonst war das Gebäude keineswegs tot – ein Kohlenhandel und diverse Firmen hatten sich behelfsmäßig dort angesiedelt.

The ruin

The gutted ruin of the palace dominated the city centre of Berlin for five years. However, not only had most of the outside walls survived the bombing, some of the rooms were still intact and usable as well. In 1946, the inhabitants of Berlin, starving for culture after Nazi dictatorship and years of war, were able to visit an exhibition of French impressionists staged in the palace's White Hall, where a presentation titled "Berlin is making plans" (*Berlin plant*) had already given the people some idea of reconstruction plans for the city. In 1948, the last exhibition to be staged at the palace glorified the centenary of the revolution. But in other aspects, too, the building was still not dead: a coal merchant and various companies had started to use the palace as their provisional headquarters.

Luftbild von 1945 | Aerial photograph taken in 1945

Ausstellung zur Märzrevolution 1848 im Weßen Saal, 1948 | Exhibition on the 1848 March Revolution, White Hall

Plakat zur Ausstellung und ... | Exhibition poster and   .... Blick in die Ausstellung „Berlin plant", 1946 | inside the exhibition "Berlin is making plans"

Frühe Planungen

1948 reiste eine Ostberliner Delegation nach Moskau, um zu analysieren, wie eine sozialistische Stadt aufgebaut ist. Dort fand man an zentraler Stelle den Roten Platz vor und kehrte mit der Erkenntnis heim, dass auch Berlin in seiner Mitte über einen derartigen Aufmarschplatz verfügen müsse. Nichts lag näher, als dies aufs Schlossareal anzuwenden, ginge damit doch die in höchstem Maße symbolische Tilgung einer für überkommen geglaubten Epoche einher. Walter Ulbricht erteilte den Befehl zur Sprengung, nachdem der obendrein geplante Abriss des Berliner Doms aufgrund internationaler Proteste ad acta gelegt worden war. Während man sich einerseits fürchtete als „Kirchenstürmer" zu gelten, hieß es indes aus Ulbrichts Kreisen, dass man mit den „paar protestierenden Kunsthistorikern schon fertig" und sicherlich bald „kein Hahn mehr nach dem Schloss krähen" werde. Jenseits der Spree, in der einstigen Altstadt, sollte nun ein Hochhaus im stalinistischen Stil entstehen, das das historische Zentrum dominiert und den eigentlichen Standort des Schlosses zu einem monumentalen Vorplatz degradiert hätte.

Early planning stages

In 1948, a delegation from East Berlin travelled to Moscow in order to analyse the layout of a socialist city. The officials were particularly impressed by Moscow's Red Square and returned to Berlin convinced that their city, too, needed similar parade grounds in its centre. The most obvious place to implement this project was the ground on which the palace stood, last but not least since this would also involve the highly symbolic end of a "bygone era". After plans to demolish the Berlin Cathedral as well had been abandoned due to international protest, Walter Ulbricht ordered demolition of the palace by controlled explosion. While, on the one hand, political leaders of the Ulbricht camp feared a reputation as "church desecrators", they were, on the other hand, convinced that it would be "no problem handling a few protesting art historians" and that soon nobody would "care two hoots about the palace". A Stalinist-style high-rise building which would dominate the historic city centre and would degrade the actual palace site to a gigantic forecourt was planned on the other side of the Spree, in the former old town.

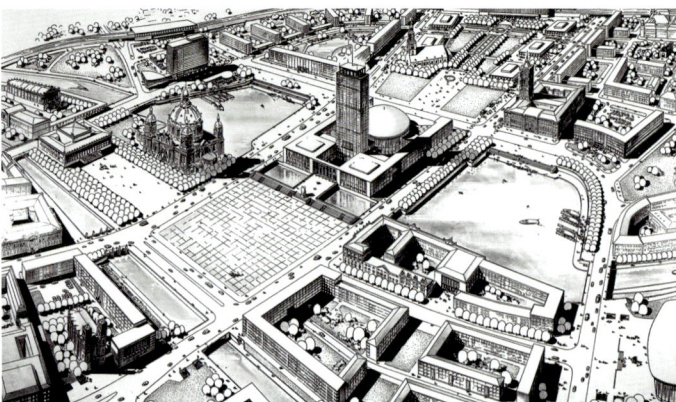

Überarbeiteter Entwurf von Kosel, Hopp und Mertens für ein Hochhaus nebst geflutetem Nikolaiviertel, 1959 |
Revised draft by Kosel, Hopp and Mertens for a high-rise building and flooded Nikolai Quarter

Entwurf für ein stalinistisches Zentralgebäude auf dem heutigen Marx-Engels-Forum von DDR-Bauminister Gerhard Kosel, 1951 |
Plans for a Stalinist-style central building on present-day Marx-Engels-Forum designed by GDR Building Minister, Gerhard Kosel

Die Vernichtung

Die Sprengung des Schlosses begann unter heftigem, doch aussichtslosem Protest im September des Jahres 1950 und erstreckte sich über drei Monate. Man schlachtete das Spektakel propagandistisch als Start in eine neue Gesellschaftsform aus. Die Trümmerberge, im Akkord abtransportiert, wurden im Volkspark Friedrichshain zu einem später begrünten Hügel aufgeschüttet, weitere Bausubstanz landete in ehemaligen Kiesgruben im Berliner Umland. Ab 1951 befand sich auf dem Schlossareal eine Tribüne, auf die sich dreimal im Jahr an hohen Festtagen die Elite der DDR drängte, um den Aufmärschen der Massen beizuwohnen. An allen anderen Tagen aber blieb das Areal öde und leer.

Destruction

Demolition of the palace started in September 1950, following fierce but futile protests, and the work lasted three months. The event was used for propaganda purposes, and was intended to symbolise the beginning of a new social order. The rubble was removed as quickly as possible and was used to form a hill that was later landscaped in the Volkspark Friedrichshain. Some of the rubble was used as backfill for former gravel pits on the outskirts of Berlin. In 1951, a platform was erected where the former palace had stood so that East Germany's elite could watch the mass parades held three times a year on important public holidays. For the remainder of the year, the site stood empty and deserted.

Schlosssprengung (7.9. bis 30.12.1950) | Demolition of the palace

Liebknecht auf Portal V des Schlosses in einer Darstellung nahezu deckungsgleich mit der Wilhelms II. (vgl. S. 25) | Liebknecht on the balcony of Portal V, depicted in an almost identical pose to that of Wilhelm II in 1914 (see p. 25)

Das „Liebknecht-Portal"

Wie eine gespenstische Kulisse stand einzig ein Teil des Nordflügels des Schlosses mit den Portalen IV und V noch bis ins Frühjahr 1951. Seine Sprengung hatte die DDR zurückgestellt, verfolgte man doch den Plan, Portal V zu bergen, um es dereinst in einem damals noch nicht näher definierten Staatsbau als Reliquie zu verwenden. Hierbei berief man sich auf den Kommunisten Karl Liebknecht, der durch seine Verkündung einer niemals Wirklichkeit gewordenen Sozialistischen Deutschen Republik am 9. November 1918 als indirekter Gründungsvater der DDR empfunden wurde. Diesen Mythos nährte ein sowjetisches Gemälde, seinerzeit Bestandteil eines nahezu jeden DDR-Schulgeschichtsbuchs, das ihn mit roter Fahne am Schlossbalkon die Menschenmenge adressierend zeigt. Es existiert kein Nachweis darüber, ob Liebknecht tatsächlich von Portal V oder nicht lediglich vom Dach eines Lastwagens vor dem Schloss gesprochen hat. Eine tiefgreifende Symbolik hätte es allemal bedient, hatte doch auch Kaiser Wilhelm II. die Mobilmachung am Anbeginn des Ersten Weltkriegs von dort proklamiert.

Am 30. Januar 1950 steht nur noch ein kleiner Teil des Schlosses. Das freigelegte Mauerwerk zeugt vom Ausbau von Portal IV | On 30 January 1950, only a small section of the palace remains. The uncovered stonework shows that Portal IV has been removed.

The "Liebknecht Portal"

Only one section of the palace's north wing comprising portals IV und V was left standing, and remained there – like a ghost of the past – until early 1951. The GDR had postponed demolition because there were plans to salvage Portal V and incorporate it as a relic into an official building yet to be defined. This measure was justified by reference to Communist leader, Karl Liebknecht. He was considered to be the indirect founding father of the GDR after proclaiming a "Free Socialist Republic" on 9 November 1918, even though this republic never became reality. The myth was nurtured by a Soviet painting which appeared in almost every East German history book, showing Liebknecht addressing the crowds from the palace balcony, from which a red flag is flying. There is no evidence that Liebknecht actually did hold his speech from the balcony above Portal V or whether he simply stood on the roof of a truck in front of the palace. All the same, the event took on a deep symbolic meaning, for this was the very same balcony where Emperor William II had proclaimed general mobilisation at the beginning of the First World War.

However, the plans to preserve Portal V did not work out. Despite being cushioned by bales of straw during demolition, the stones shattered into tiny pieces that could

Portal V und IV am Schloss (oben) und Portal IV, das sogenannte Liebknecht-Portal, am Staatsratsgebäude (unten) |
Portals V and IV of the palace (above) and Portal IV, the so-called Liebknecht Portal, of the Staatsratsgebäude (below)

42

Doch das Vorhaben, Portal V zu konservieren, misslang. Ließ man es bei dessen Sprengung zwar auf vorsorglich ausgelegte Strohmatten fallen, zerbarst es trotzdem in nicht mehr verwendbare Bruchstücke. Portal IV war zu diesem Zeitpunkt noch unzerstört, also baute man ersatzweise nun dieses minutiös aus und münzte es, aufgrund der Ähnlichkeit beider, kurzerhand zum „Original-Liebknecht-Portal" um – in der Hoffnung, keiner würde den Unterschied bemerken.

Doch auch das falsche Portal fand nur bedingt Verwendung. Bei Baubeginn des Staatsratsgebäudes 1961, nur einen Steinwurf vom ehemaligen Schloss entfernt, besah sich Staatschef Walter Ulbricht die zehn Jahre zuvor geborgenen Teile. Diese waren nicht nur durch die Endkämpfe des Jahres 1945 mit Einschusslöchern übersät, schon 1918 war das Portal in den Revolutionstagen beschossen und beschädigte Bereiche durch Steine ohne die alte Patina ersetzt worden. Ulbricht aber wünschte, dass ein unversehrtes Portal den Eingang zum Staatsrat bildete, und entschied, nahezu die gesamte Fassade neu fertigen zu lassen. Doch selbst die wenigen wiederverwandten Spolien wurden nachträglich modifiziert, so tilgte man unter anderem den Adler aus dem Wappenschild über der Serliana und entfernte auch die aufsitzende Krone.

Noch heute hält sich die Legende vom sozialistisch geweihten, originalen Liebknecht-Portal im nunmehr denkmalgeschützten Staatsratsgebäude hartnäckig. Dass es sich nicht nur um das falsche Portal, sondern weitestgehend um dessen vereinfachte Replik ohne preußische Insignien handelt, erinnern dagegen die wenigsten.

Die Serliana an Portal IV des Schlosses ... | Serliana over Portal IV of the palace

Portal IV auf der Lustgartenseite des Schlosses ... | Portal IV on the palace façade facing the Lustgarten

...und am Staatsratgebäude ohne Krone und Adler | and over the State Council Building without crown and eagle

no longer be re-used. At this time, Portal IV was still intact, and so this was meticulously taken down instead. Since the two portals looked very much alike, Portal IV was declared without further ado to be the "original Liebknecht portal", in the hope that no-one would notice the difference.

But even the "false" portal was only used to a certain degree. When construction work was commenced on the Staatsratsgebäude in 1961, just a stone's throw away from the former palace, East German head of state, Walter Ulbricht, decided to take a closer look at the parts salvaged ten years ago. These were not only covered in bullet holes like most buildings after the final battle for Berlin in 1945, the portal had already been the target of shooting during the 1918 uprising and the damaged sections had been replaced by stones which did not display the original patina. Ulbricht, however, wanted an undamaged portal to form the entrance to the State Council building and so he ordered reconstruction of almost the entire façade. Even the few spolias that were selected for re-use were modified: for example the eagle was removed from the coat of arms above the Serlian window and also the crown mounted on top of this had to go.

Even today, the socialistic legend of the original Liebknecht portal forming the entrance to the Staatsratsgebäude, now declared a historical monument, dies hard. There are few people who actually remember that this is not only the wrong portal, but that it is more or less just a simplified replica of the original, without the Prussian insignia.

...und als zentraler Eingang des Staatsratsgebäudes am Schlossplatz | and as main entrance to the State Council Building

Lustgarten, Dom und Schloss, dahinter das Heilig-Geist- und Marienviertel, um 1910 |
Lustgarten, cathedral and palace, in the background the Heilig-Geist and Marien Quarters, around 1910

Die U-förmige Staatsmitte der DDR

Mit dem Staatsratsgebäude war der Grundstein für ein völlig neues Konzept zur sozialistischen Umgestaltung der Berliner Mitte gelegt. Der Architekturgeschmack hatte sich nach Stalins Tod zunehmend in eine andere Richtung entwickelt, und die Errichtung eines Zentralgebäudes im Zuckerbäckerstil, bis dato ein ums andere Mal vertagt, erschien nun unzeitgemäß. Zur Umsetzung kam stattdessen ein nach Norden geöffnetes u-förmiges Staatsforum bestehend aus Staatsratsgebäude (1961 bis 1963), Außenministerium (1964 bis 1967) und Palast der Republik (1973 bis 1976). Beim Bau des

Palastes, welcher die Volkskammer der DDR beherbergen würde, gleichzeitig aber auch ein Haus des Volkes sein sollte, belebt durch Gastronomie und Veranstaltungssäle, wurden die sich um den einstigen Schlüterhof herum befindlichen Kellermauern des Schlosses ohne jedwede Form der Dokumentation aus dem Erdreich entfernt. Vor dem Palast der Republik sollte erneut ein Paradeplatz entstehen – überbaute der Palast doch nur etwa die Hälfte des einstigen Schlossgrundrisses. Unter dieser asphaltierten Fläche blieben die Kellerreste um den westlich gelegenen Eosanderhof über Jahrzehnte im Erdreich konserviert.

Funktionierende Telefone, neumodische Kegelbahnen, Konzerte von Stars aus Ost und West – darunter Harry Belafonte und Udo Lindenberg – sowie eine ausgeklügelte Bühnentechnik in einem Veranstaltungssaal, der zu dieser Zeit seinesgleichen suchte, erfreuten die Ostberliner und ihre Gäste. Doch auch Verstörendes prägte das Bild: Besuchern mit Westwährung gewährte man bevorzugten Einlass, über Wanzen, nicht nur in den Salz- und Pfefferstreuern des Restaurants, observierte man die Gäste. Der Palast der Republik wurde im Jahr 1990 durch die letzte DDR-Regierung aufgrund seiner nun publik gewordenen Asbestbelastung geschlossen.

DDR-Staatsforum bestehend aus Palast der Republik, Staatsratsgebäude und Außenministerium, 1995 |
GDR State Forum: Palace of the Republic, State Council Building and Ministry of Foreign Affairs

East Germany's U-shaped political centre

The Staatsratsgebäude was the cornerstone of a totally new concept for a socialist transformation of Berlin's centre. After Stalin's death, architectural tastes began to change and the idea of a Stalinist-style high-rise building as the city's focal point, a project that had been repeatedly postponed, now seemed out of keeping with the times. Instead of this, the concept of a U-shaped state forum was implemented. This opened towards the north and comprised the State Council Building (Staatsratsgebäude 1961 – 1963), the Ministry of Foreign Affairs (1964 – 1967) and the Palace of the Republic (1973 – 1976). When the Palace of the Republic (Palast der Republik) was built, the former basement walls around the Schlüter Courtyard were removed without being documented. The new building housed East Germany's People's Chamber and was intended to be used as a popular culture centre (Haus des Volkes), with a restaurant and multi-purpose halls for events; a new parade ground was to be created in front of it since the actual building only covered around half the area of the former Berlin Palace. For decades, the remains of the basement walls of the buildings around the west-facing Eosander Courtyard were preserved underneath this asphalted surface. East Berlin citizens and their guests enjoyed the pleasures of telephones that worked, modern bowling alleys and concerts by stars from both east and west – including Harry Belafonte and Udo Lindenberg – held at a concert hall with sophisticated stage technology that was second to none at the time. This "beauty" was only skin deep, however: Visitors who paid in western currencies were privileged when it came to obtaining tickets and there were microphones hidden everywhere – even in the restaurants' salt and pepper shakers – to keep a check on guests. The Palast der Republik was closed down by the last East German government in 1990 after it had become publicly known that the building was contaminated with asbestos.

Lindenblick auf den Palast der Republik ... | Palast der Republik seen from Unter den Linden

Debatten der Nachwendezeit

Nach 1990 war kein anderer Ort der nun wiedervereinten Stadt so heftig umkämpft, so umworben, wie der Standort des einstigen Schlosses. Von Anfang an war offensichtlich, dass nichts so bleiben konnte, wie es war – stellte das u-förmige Staatsforum der DDR doch einen städtebaulichen Affront dar. Der Palast der Republik, ungeachtet seiner architektonischen Qualitäten, riegelte die Stadt nach Osten wie eine undurchdringliche Wand ab. Der einstmals als Aufmarschfläche konzipierte Vorplatz, Kulminationspunkt der Straße Unter den Linden, präsentierte sich dem Be-trachter nun als banaler Park-platz. Am störendsten emp-fand man aber wohl, wie das Außenministerium der DDR die historischen Bauten Unter den Linden überragte. Sang und klanglos, ohne nennens-werte Proteste, baute man es in den Neunzigerjahren zu-rück. Das Staats-U war fortan kein U mehr, das DDR-Ensem-ble aufgebrochen.

Oft hört man noch heute, die Asbestbelastung des Palas-tes sei als Vorwand genutzt worden, ihn im Zuge einer Siegermentalität über die untergegangene DDR zu be-seitigen, ähnlich wie es die DDR mit dem Schloss zuvor getan hatte. Tatsächlich ent-schied das Nachwende-Ber-lin sehr früh, das nahegele-gene Staatsratsgebäude, die Keimzelle des DDR-Staats-apparates, unter Denkmal-schutz zu stellen. Auch der Fernsehturm, die von weither unübersehbare Stadtdomi-nante des Sozialismus, stand niemals zur Disposition. So war es letztlich nicht der Asbest, sondern die städte-baulichen Defizite des Pa-lastes, die seinen Untergang einläuteten. Das von Senats-baudirektor Hans Stimmann initiierte *Planwerk Innenstadt* sah bereits in den ersten Nachwendejahren auch im Bereich des Palastes die Wie-dergewinnung vergangener Strukturen vor. Eine Neupla-nung im Sinne der „europä-ischen Stadt" sollte es sein

Marstall mit Palast der Republik | Marstall and Palast der Republik

Das Kronprinzenpalais überragt vom DDR-Außenministerium | Ministry of Foreign Affairs towers over Kronprinzenpalais

– dichter, auf ein menschli-ches Maß zurückgeführt, in Referenz an alte Strukturen, aber mit den Mitteln gänzlich zeitgenössischer Architektur. Ein Rückgriff auf ein altes Ge-bäude in einer Stadt, die sich so unaufhaltsam der Zukunft verschrieben hatte wie Berlin, schien zu diesem Zeitpunkt nicht ins Bild zu passen.

… Lindenblick aufs rekonstruierte Berliner Schloss | reconstructed Berlin Palace seen from Unter den Linden

Marstall mit Schloss |
Marstall and palace

Abriss Außenministerium, 1995 |
Demolition of the Ministry of Foreign Affairs

Post-reunification discussions

In the years after 1990, no other piece of land in the reunited city was as highly coveted as the site of the former Berlin Palace. It was obvious right from the start that things could not stay as they were, since East Berlin's U-shaped state forum was a veritable insult to urban development. Despite having cer-tain architectural qualities, the Palast der Republik blocked off the eastern part of the city like an impervious wall. The large forecourt – originally de-signed as a parade ground – which marked the end of Unter den Linden was now no more than a plain parking lot. Ber-lin's decision-makers, however, seemed to consider the Min-istry of Foreign Affairs, which towered over the historic build-ings of Unter den Linden, to be the most disturbing edi-fice. It was torn down in the nineties, without further ado and with no protest worth mentioning. The state forum had lost its U-shape, East Ber-lin's architectural ensemble had been broken apart.

Some people still argue to-day that contamination with asbestos was just used as an excuse to tear down the Palast der Republik as a sign of vic-tory over the now-extinct Ger-man Democratic Republic, in the same way as the GDR had demolished the City Palace many years ago. As a matter of fact, very soon after reunifi-cation, the Berlin monument protection authority declared the nearby Staatsratsgebäude, the hub of the East German government machinery, to be a listed monument. Tearing down the Berlin TV Tower, the most conspicuous and domi-nant building of the Socialist era, was never an option, either. So, ultimately, it was not asbes-tos but the building's urban planning deficiencies that put the final nail in the coffin of the Palast der Republik. The Inner city plan (*Planwerk Innenstadt*), initiated by Director of the Sen-ate Department of Urban De-velopment, Hans Stimmann, in the first years following reuni-fication already included plans to recover historic structures on the site of the former Berlin Pal-ace. The concept was to rede-velop the area as a "European City" – more dense, cut back to a human scale, with reference to old structures but using the means of modern architecture. At the time, recourse to an old building in a city which had dedicated itself to the future as relentlessly as Berlin had did not fit into the picture.

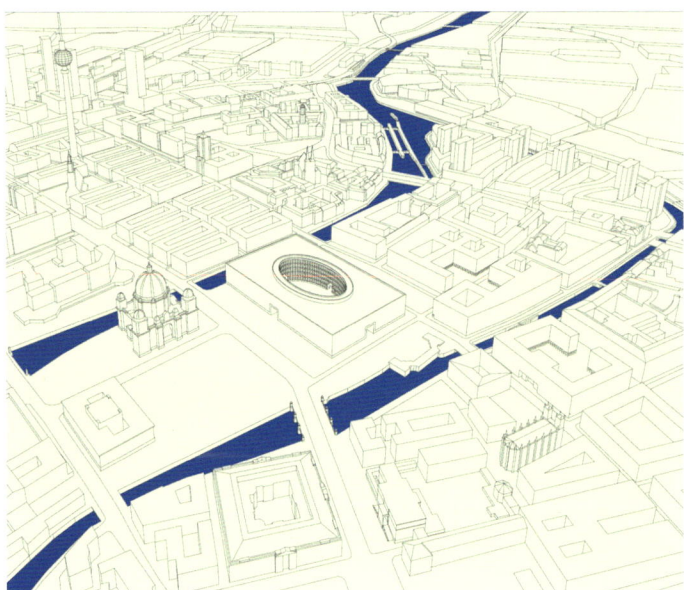

Siegerentwurf „Spreeinsel-Wettbewerb" | Winning design "Spree island competition", Bernd Niebuhr, 1994

Ein moderner Neubau schien also bereits ausgemachte Sache. 1994 ging Architekt Bernd Niebuhr mit einem zeitgenössischen Gebäude, auffällig durch seinen charakteristischen ovalen Innenhof, aus einem *Ideenwettbewerb Spreeinsel* als Sieger hervor. Und auch an Alternativideen mangelte es nicht. Sei es die komplette Neuordnung des Areals wie Axel Schultes und Charlotte Frank sie vorschlugen oder eine Halb-Schloss-Halb-Palast-Variante, der Diskussionsbeitrag Wolf-Rüdiger Borchardt. Bolles + Wilson zäumten das Pferd von hinten auf: Statt einer Fassadenwiederherstellung gedachten sie lediglich, rekonstruierte Innenräume, von Stelzen getragen, auf den Schlossplatz zu setzen. Über Jahre hinweg kursierten, fernab von Wettbewerben, immer neue Entwürfe durch die Medien. Der große Wurf war freilich nicht dabei. Und die Frage blieb: Konnte man die Geschichte dieses Ortes so einfach negieren oder hatte das Schloss vielleicht sogar ein Anrecht auf diesen Platz?

It therefore appeared to be an open and shut case in favour of a new, modern building. In 1994, architect Bernd Niebuhr won first prize in a competition of ideas for the Spree island and presented a contemporary building characterised by a striking oval courtyard. But there was no lack of alternative ideas. Axel Schultes and Charlotte Frank, for example, suggested complete re-arrangement of the site, and Wolf-Rüdiger Borchardt suggested a semi-reconstructed baroque palace in front of the preserved Palast der Republik. Bolles + Wilson, on the other hand, put the cart before the horse: Instead of rebuilding the façade, they suggested placing some reconstructed rooms – supported by stilts – on Palace Square. Numerous other new designs emerged in the media over the years, beyond any competitions. Admittedly, none of these was the big scoop. And so the question remained: Was it acceptable to simply negate the history of this site or did the palace perhaps have a legitimate claim to be there?

Modell | Model Bernd Niebuhr, 1994

Entwurf von Axel Schultes und Charlotte Frank | design by Axel Schultes und Charlotte Frank

Entwurf von | design by W.-R. Borchardt

Entwurf von | design by Bolles + Wilson

Schlossattrappe, Juni 1993 | Palace simulation, June 1993

Die Schlossattrappe

In den Jahren 1993 und 1994 initiierte der *Förderverein Berliner Schloss* um den Hamburger Landmaschinenhändler Wilhelm von Boddien die sogenannte „Schlossattrappe" – ein genialer Coup, der als Initialzündung fungieren sollte. Ein mit Planen behängtes Gerüst beförderte das aus den Köpfen der Berliner verschwundene Schloss in die Jetztzeit zurück. Die eindrucksvolle Präsentation bildete die originären Ausmaße der Fassade, wo dies möglich war, an ursprünglicher Stelle ab. Den Palast der Republik hatte man gen Westen mit einer verspielten Gerüstwand verstellt, dadurch entstand der Eindruck, die Fassadensimulation setze sich nach Osten hin zur vollen Länge des Schlosses fort. Historiker Joachim Fest, Verleger Wolf Jobst Siedler, Politiker Wolfgang Thierse – sie und viele andere gaben sich im Zuge dieser Installation als Unterstützer der Idee zu erkennen, Berlin die Schönheit seiner einstigen Mitte zurückzugeben. Doch es formierte sich auch Widerstand gegen die erstmals in Betracht gezogene Möglichkeit eines Wiederaufbaus. Etliche zeitgenössische Architekten wurden nicht müde, Rekonstruktion per se als etwas „Unanständiges" und „Unehrliches" zu diffamieren – in völliger Missachtung der Tatsache, dass nicht nur seit Kriegsende in Europa und anderswo Rekonstruktion als sehr erfolgreiches Mittel genutzt worden war, zerstörten Städten ihr Gesicht zurückzugeben. Eine Phalanx an Journalisten verwechselte obendrein die Wiederkehr eines intakten Stadtbildes mit dem reaktionären Wiederauflebenlassen einer überkommen geglaubten Epoche. Eine Debatte, die weit über die Stadtgrenzen hinausgehen und nahezu zehn Jahre anhalten sollte, war entbrannt.

Palace simulation

In 1993 and 1994, the Förder-verein Berliner Schloss e.V. (Association Berliner Schloss) founded and chaired by Ham-burg business man, Wilhelm von Boddien, initiated the installa-tion of a so-called palace simu-lation – a brilliant idea aimed at paving the way for reconstruc-tion of the Berlin Palace. Scaf-folding covered with canvas brought the palace, which Ber-liners had more or less forgot-ten in the meantime, back to life. The impressive presenta-tion showed the façade in its original dimensions and at the original location, as far as pos-sible. The west side of the Palast der Republik was covered over with a mirrored scaffolding wall, giving viewers the impres-sion that the mock-up façade continued eastwards over the full length of the palace. In the course of this installation, his-torian Joachim Fest, publisher Wolf Jobst Siedler, politician Wolfgang Thierse and many others outed themselves as supporters of the idea to restore Berlin's city centre to its former beauty. At the same time, op-position began to grow against proposals to rebuild the palace – an idea never seriously con-sidered before. Several contem-porary architects never tired of demonising the reconstruction as being "improper" and "dis-honest" – completely ignoring the fact that reconstruction had already proven to be a success-ful way of giving destroyed cit-ies their identity back – not only since the war, and not only in Europe but in other parts of the world as well. Furthermore, a phalanx of journalists confused the attempt to restore the city-scape with a reactionary resur-rection of an era believed to be gone for good. A lively debate which extended far beyond the city limits and lasted for almost ten years had been sparked off.

Abbau der Simulation, 1994 | Removal of the simulated façade

Die Expertenkommission

Im Jahre 2000 schließlich gelang es der Bundesregierung und dem Berliner Senat, die anhaltende Auseinandersetzung in produktive Bahnen zu lenken. Man lud 17 internationale Experten nach Berlin ein, die unter dem Vorsitz von Hannes Swoboda, ehemaliger Städteplaner aus Wien, ergebnisoffen über die künftige Nutzung und den Umgang mit dem einstigen Schlossareal berieten und mit einer Empfehlung an die politischen Entscheider aufwarten sollten. Deren Analyse zeigte sehr schnell, wie maßgeblich das Schloss, der erste Bau am Platze, sein Umfeld geprägt hatte. Nicht zuletzt Raschdorffs massiver Dom ist ohne die Schlosskuppel als sein Gegengewicht nicht zu verstehen. Schinkels Altes Museum, dessen Architektur die Agora Athens nachempfindet, und damit auf die älteste Demokratie der Geschichte verweist, ist als heftiger Kontrast zu einem Monarchensitz in Abwesenheit des Schlosses nicht nachvollziehbar. Die Liste auf das Schloss hin komponierter, mit der Fassade eng verzahnter Gebäude ließe sich fortsetzen.

In ihrer Empfehlung an die Politik votierten 15 Kommissionsmitglieder für einen Neubau in der Kubatur des einstigen Schlosses an ursprünglicher Stelle. Acht zu sieben stimmte man für die Rekonstruktion der barocken Außenfassaden und des Schlüterhofs. Die Ausgestaltung der nichtbarocken Bereiche wurde für einen später auszulotenden Architekturwettbewerb offengehalten. Um dieses Ergebnis einer Teilrekonstruktion nachvollziehen zu können, lohnt es sich, im Folgenden die betreffenden Stadträume näher zu untersuchen.

The committee of experts

In 2000, the government of the Federal Republic of Germany and the Senate of Berlin finally managed to bring the ongoing debate back onto a constructive track. Seventeen international experts were invited to Berlin to form an expert committee chaired by Hannes Swoboda, a former city planner from Vienna, and to discuss the future of the plot of land where the palace had stood. This discussion was to be open and unbiased and produce recommendations for presentation to political decision-makers. The experts' analysis soon showed how much the palace, the first building constructed on the site, had influenced its surroundings. Raschdorff's gigantic Berlin Cathedral in particular appears totally out of context without the palace dome as a counterpart. Also, Schinkel's Altes Museum, the design of which is based on the Agora in Athens in reference to history's oldest democracy, loses its meaning unless the palace – the residence of kings and emperors – is there as a contrast. The list of other buildings designed in composition with the palace and with close design links to its façade is long.

In their recommendations, fifteen members of the committee voted for a new building with the same cubature as the former palace and on the original site. Eight experts voted for and seven against reconstruction of the baroque outer façade and the Schlüter Courtyard. The exact design of the non-baroque areas was to be decided later in an architectural competition. It is worthwhile taking a closer look at the urban spaces in question in order to understand why the experts came to the conclusion that parts the palace should be reconstructed.

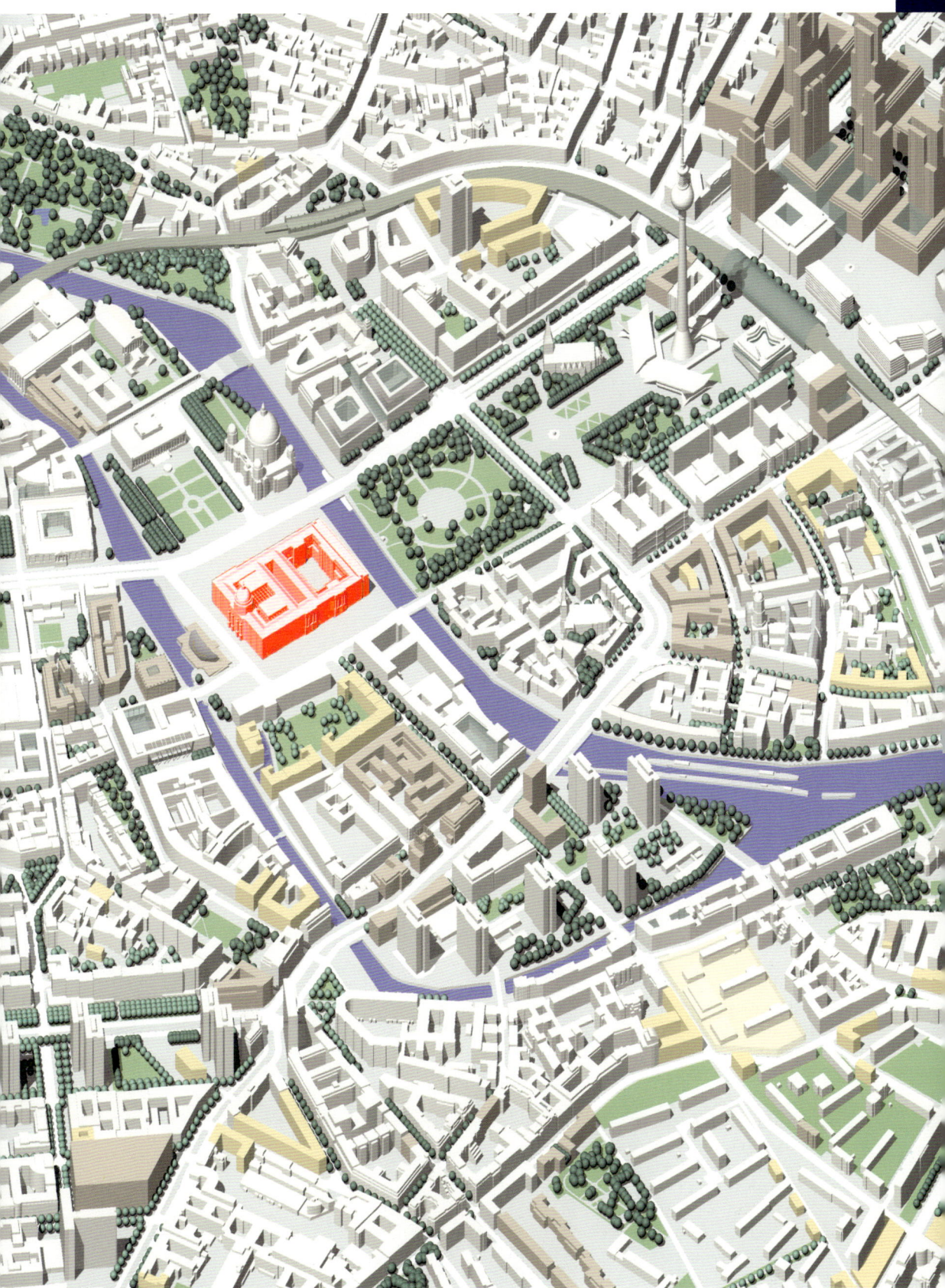

Nach Kriegsende ist die vom Schloss ausgehende Stadtmitte in drei Himmelsrichtungen nahezu originalgetreu rekonstruiert worden. In den Fünfzigerjahren hatte man das Forum Fridericianum mit Knobelsdorffs Oper, Kommode und Universität wiederaufgebaut, ebenso Zeughaus und Marstall. Die Wiedereröffnung des Alten Museums erfolgte im Jahre 1966, die Totalrekonstruktion des Kronprinzenpalais ab 1969, die Instandsetzung des Doms zwischen 1975 und 1983. Die Rekonstruktion der einstigen Kommandantur reichte Bertelsmann im Jahre 2003 nach, einzig die Bauakademie steht noch aus. Sukzessive hatte sich das Vorkriegsstadtbild regeneriert, nach und nach waren die einst aufs Schloss hin komponierten Gebäude zurückgekehrt – jedoch nur auf einer Seite der Spree.

After the end of WW II, the city centre was reconstructed almost true to the original in three directions. The Forum Fridericianum, comprising Knobelsdorff's opera, the Kommode and the university, was rebuilt in the 1950s, as were the Zeughaus and the Marstall. The Altes Museum was reopened in 1966, total reconstruction of the Kronprinzenpalais was commenced in 1969 and the Berlin Cathedral was restored between 1975 and 1983. The Bertelsmann media group financed reconstruction of the Alte Kommandantur in 2003. The Bauakademie is the only building which has not yet been rebuilt. The cityscape has gradually been restored to the way it was before the war, buildings which were once designed in harmony with the palace have returned, one by one – but only on one side of the Spree.

Wiederaufbau Oper | Rebuilding the opera house

Prinzessinnenpalais zerstört … | Prinzessinnenpalais is destroyed

…und rekonstruiert. | and rebuilt.

Erhaltene bzw. rekonstruierte Vorkriegsbausubstanz westlich und östlich des Schlosses (rot) |

Instandsetzung des Berliner Doms | Restoration of Berlin Cathedral

Errichtung der Wohnscheiben am Rathausforum, 1969 | Prefabricated apartments, Rathausforum

Östlich des einstigen Schlosses, im ältesten Teil der Stadt, war Ende der Sechzigerjahre eine DDR-Moderne etabliert worden, die auf historische Gegebenheiten keinerlei Rücksicht nahm. Straßenverläufe wurden verschwenkt und radikal verbreitert, das Rathausforum mit seinen Wohnhausscheiben entstand, dazwischen erhob sich der Fernsehturm. Marienkirche und Rotes Rathaus überlebten als bloße Rudimente auf diesem vollkommen neugeordneten Areal. Selbst das bis 1987 wiederaufgebaute Nikolaiviertel präsentiert sich in nördlicher Richtung in gänzlich moderner Architektur. Es handelt sich just um jenen Stadtraum, in den auch die Ostseite des wiederaufgebauten Schlosses zeigen würde – welche im Falle einer Rekonstruktion nun deplaziert auf eine Formsprache verweisen würde, die dem Stadtraum in keiner Weise mehr entspricht.

Retained/rebuilt pre-war buildings east and west of the palace (in red)

Marienkirche und Fernsehturm, um 1980 | Marienkirche and TV Tower around 1980

To the east of the former palace, in the oldest part of the city, East German modern design had established itself by the late 1960s. This took no consideration of historical structures whatsoever. Streets and roads were rerouted and radically widened, the Rathausforum, consisting of prefabricated apartment blocks, was built, and in the middle of all this, the television tower. The Marienkirche and the Rotes Rathaus are the only remnants of prewar Berlin in this completely restructured area. Modern architecture has also taken over to the north of the Nikolai Quarter, reconstruction of which was completed in 1987. This is precisely that urban space which would face the east façade of a reconstructed palace – and if this were to be rebuilt in its original style, it would look completely out of place.

Nikolaiviertel mit modernem Nordabschluss, 2016 | Nikolai Quarter and modern buildings to the north

Die Empfehlung

Das Berliner Schloss war nie ein Gebäude aus einem Guss. Es fungierte stets als Scharnier zwischen barocker Stadt im Westen und dem mittelalterlichem Grundriss im Osten. Die Rekonstruktion der drei barocken Außenfassaden repariert das Stadtbild in drei Himmelsrichtungen und stellt die Bezüge zu den Bauten ringsum wieder her.

The recommendation

The Berlin Palace had never been a homogeneous building. It had always been the hinge between a baroque town to the west and a medieval layout to the east. Re construction of the three baroque outer façades will restore the cityscape in three directions and re-establish the relationship between the palace and its surrounding buildings.

Der *Lynartrakt* – Schlüter selbst wollte ihn schon abreißen und durch barocke Architektur ersetzen – wurde als nicht rekonstruktionswürdig empfunden. Er ist als Rudiment des Renaissanceschlosses zu betrachten. Seine Architektur findet sich in den Stadträumen ringsum nicht wieder.

The experts considered that it was not worthwhile reconstructing the *Lynar wing* – which Schlüter himself had intended to tear down and replace by baroque architecture. This must be regarded as a remnant of the renaissance palace. Its architecture does not reflect that of the surrounding urban spaces.

Die *Wasserseite* mit ihrem kleinteiligen Mix aus Mittelalter- und Renaissancearchitektur war nie durch einen barocken Abschluss ersetzt worden und bildete damit das Pendant zum altstädtischen Gegenüber. Doch warum heute erneut den Übergang zu einem Stadtraum gestalten, der gegenwärtig gar nicht mehr existiert, und zwischenzeitlich vollkommen neu definiert wurde? Man empfahl eine moderne Gestaltung als Bindeglied zur vorhandenen Architektur östlich der Spree. Das Schloss wird damit erneut zu einem Scharnier – diesmal zwischen barockem und modernem Stadtraum.

The waterfront façade with its fragmented combination of renaissance and medieval architecture had never been replaced by baroque architecture and formed a counterpart to the "old town" architecture on the other side of the river. But why should the connec-

Das Schloss wird keine Kulisse sein: Auch der *Kleine Schlosshof*, Schlüters opus magnum, wird mit seinen drei barocken Seiten minutiös wiederhergestellt.

The palace will not be a stage set: The *Small Palace Courtyard (Kleiner Schlosshof)*, Schlüter's opus magnum, and the three baroque façades surrounding it will also be reconstructed right down to the last detail.

tion to an urban space that no longer exists and has been given a totally new definition in the meantime be restored? The committee recommended a modern design for the waterfront side as a link to the existing architecture to the east of the Spree. The palace would again become a hinge – this time between baroque and modern urban spaces.

Den *Eosanderhof*, der kunsthistorisch weniger bedeutsame der beiden Höfe, stellte die Kommission komplett zur Überbauung frei. Das neue Gebäude sollte über 40.000 Quadratmeter Nutzfläche verfügen – fast doppelt soviel wie der Ursprungsbau. Der überbaute Große Schlosshof würde diese Fläche bereitstellen.

The committee recommended that the entire area of the *Eosander Courtyard (Eosanderhof)*, which is the courtyard of lesser importance to art history, should be built up. The new building should have a usable floor space of more than 40,000 square metres – nearly twice that of the original building. The Greater Palace Courtyard (Grosser Schlosshof) would be able to provide this space.

Der Wettbewerb und sein Siegerentwurf

Am 4. Juli 2002 hatte der Deutsche Bundestag die Empfehlung der Experten-kommission angenommen und mit großer Mehrheit be-schlossen. Fünfundachtzig Architekturbüros nahmen am daraufhin 2007 ausgelobten Wettbewerbsverfahren teil. Die Rekonstruktion der baro-cken Außenfassade und des Schlüterhofs waren als Vorga-be verbindlich. Wer davon ab-wich, schied umgehend aus.

Die Wahl fiel auf einen bis dato weitgehend Unbekann-ten. Franco Stella, Architek-turprofessor aus Vicenza, er-rang den ersten Preis. Die Jury war von seinem Entwurf der-art angetan, dass kein zweiter Platz vergeben wurde, was die Wertschätzung seines Vorschlags seitens der Akteu-re zusätzlich unterstrich.

Finanzieren würde das Bau-vorhaben der Bund mit 478 Millionen Euro, Berlin würde 32 Millionen beisteuern. Die Rekonstruktion der Fassaden hingegen sollte ausschließlich über private Spenden erfol-gen. Der Steuerzahler würde nicht mit dem Mehraufwand der Wiederherstellung baro-cken Schmucks belastet wer-den. Der *Förderverein Berliner Schloss* um Wilhelm von Bod-dien machte es sich folglich zur Aufgabe, ein Spendenziel von 105 Millionen Euro zu er-reichen.

Ansicht von Nordwesten | View from the northwest

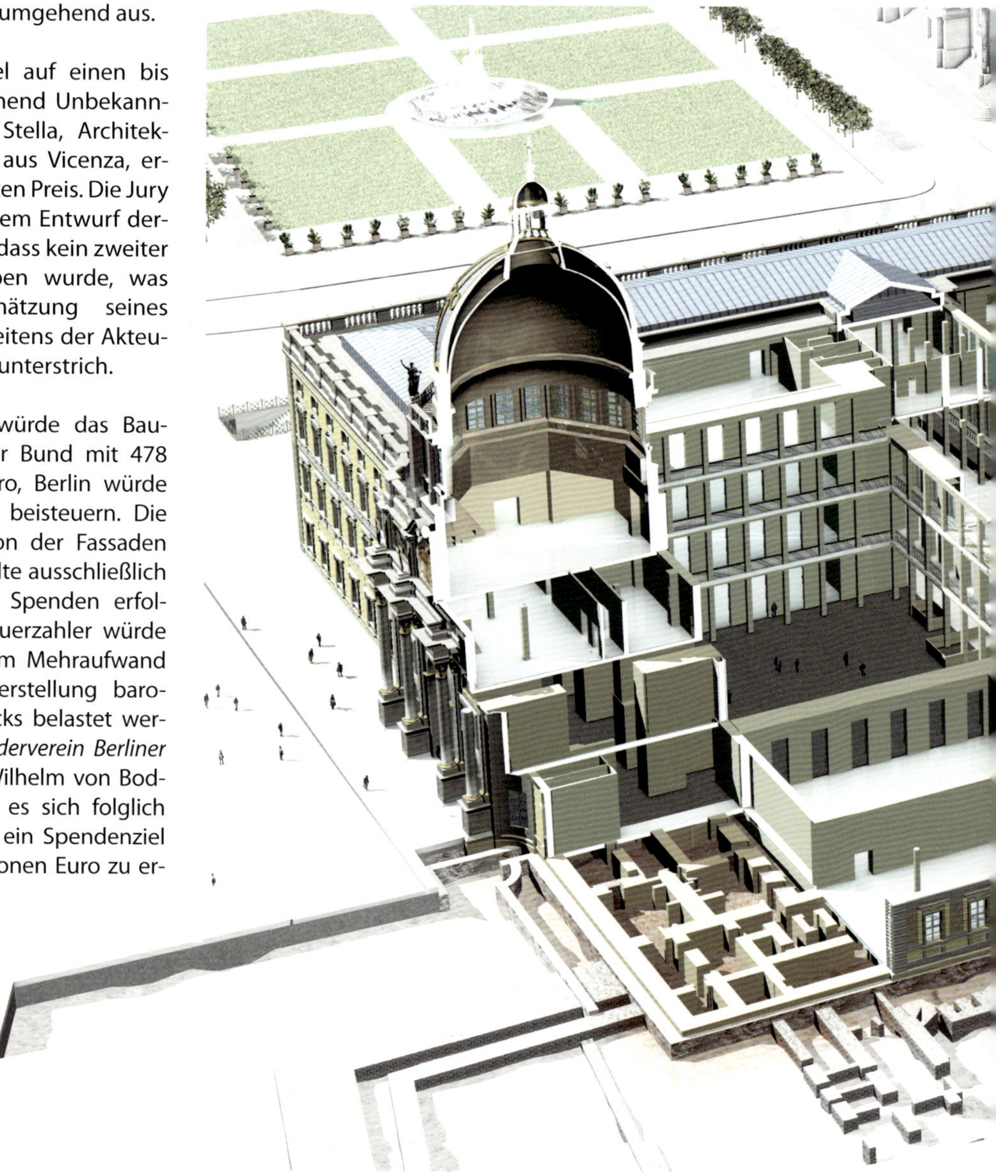

Aufriss des Neubaus: überdachtes Foyer (links), öffentliche Passage (Mitte), rekonstruierter Schlüterhof (rechts). Im Vordergrund das künftige Archäologische Fenster. | Cutaway view of new building: covered foyer (l.), open passageway (c.), reconstructed Schlüter Courtyard (r.). At the front, the planned archeological window.

The competition and the winning design

On 4th July 2002, the German Bundestag approved the expert committee's recommendation and adopted it with a clear majority. Eighty-five architects participated in the competition, which was initiated in 2007. Reconstruction of the baroque outer façades and the Schlüter courtyard was a mandatory requirement. Participants who failed to meet this were immediately excluded.

Winner of the competition was a hitherto relatively unknown architect. Franco Stella, Professor of Architecture from Vicenza, won the first prize. The jury was so impressed by his design that no second prize was awarded. This showed how highly the members valued Stella's plans.

The Federal State agreed to contribute 478 million euros and the City State of Berlin 32 million euros to the project. Reconstruction of the façades, however, was to be financed exclusively from private donations. Taxpayers were assured that they would not have to bear the additional financial burden of restoring the baroque ornaments. The *Förderverein Berliner Schloss*, chaired by Wilhelm von Boddien, consequently took on the task of raising funds totalling 105 million euros for this purpose.

Zwischen Portal II und IV schafft Stella einen tags wie nachts passierbaren Durchgang – das Gebäude wird damit vierundzwanzig Stunden durchlässig. Clou seiner Planung ist es, die Innenseiten der Portale, die einstmals in den Großen Schlosshof führten – und welche als Rekonstruktionsbereiche gar nicht gefordert waren – als Stirnseiten der Passage an ursprünglicher Stelle ebenfalls wiederherzustellen. So wird ein größtenteils vordefiniertes Gebäude in seiner Infrastruktur so umgenutzt, dass die vorhandenen Portale in neue Sinnzusammenhänge gestellt werden und das Bauwerk, der neuen Nutzung entsprechend, völlig neu erschließen.

Stella's design includes a pedestrian passageway between Portal II and Portal IV which is to be open to the public day and night – thus making the building accessible twenty-four hours a day. The highlight of his plan is a reconstruction, at the original locations, of the inner sides of the portals which formerly led into the Greater Palace Courtyard, now to create the end faces of the passageway – even though these portals had not been specified as mandatory reconstruction features. Thus, the infrastructure of a largely predefined building is to be used in a way which gives the existing portals a new context and makes the building accessible in a novel manner which is in line with its new purpose.

Zentrales Treppenhaus | Central stairway

Mittelpassage | Centre passageway

Im Bereich des ehemaligen Eosanderhofs – welcher im Vergleich zum Ursprungsbau auf einen kubischen Lichthof verengt wird –, schafft Stella eine großzügige Empfangshalle, gesäumt von Galerien, die das ebenfalls rekonstruierte Innenportal III umstellen. Dieser lichtdurchflutete, wettergeschützte Raum kann sowohl als Foyer, wie auch als Veranstaltungssaal, bestuhlbar für eintausend Personen, dienen. Das rekonstruierte Innenportal böte hierbei den spektakulären Bühnenhintergrund einer Veranstaltung. Durch die zusätzliche Erreichbarkeit des zentralen Treppenhauses über die Mittelpassage wird obendrein gewährleistet, dass der tägliche Betrieb nicht beeinträchtigt wird, wenn das Foyer von einer Veranstaltung in Beschlag genommen wird.

Where the Eosander Courtyard used to be, Stella's design envisages a spacious lobby as well as the reconstructed Portal III, both surrounded by galleries. Compared with the original, the actual courtyard is reduced in size and takes on the form of a cubic atrium. This well-lit, covered area can be used either as a foyer or as an event venue with seating for up to a thousand people. The reconstructed courtyard portal would be a spectacular stage setting for events. The fact that the central staircase is also accessible via the middle passageway ensures that daily operations are not affected when the foyer is being used as an event venue.

© FRANCO STELLA **HUF PG** / Jan Pautzke 2014

Eingangshalle | Entrance hall

Im *Lapidarium* werden künftig die noch vorhandenen Fassadenfragmente des alten Schlosses, welche nicht mehr an ihrer ursprünglichen Stelle verbaut werden können, museal präsentiert. Schlüters Gigantentreppe, die sich einst hier befand, wird nichtsdestotrotz zentimetergenau eingemessen. Sie, wie auch die barocken Prachträume des Paradegeschosses darüber (darunter der Schweizer- und Rittersaal), könnten rekonstruiert werden, wenn dies einst finanzierbar sein sollte. Derzeit gibt es keinerlei dahingehende Planungen, die längerfristige Option hierfür ist aber gegeben.

Lapidarium

Those fragments of the old palace's façade which it was not possible to reinstall at their original location will be on display at the *Lapidarium*. Nevertheless, enough space is provided for Schlüter's Giant Staircase, which used to stand here. The winning design provides an option for subsequent reconstruction of the staircase and the magnificent baroque "parade chambers" (including the Swiss Hall and the Knights' Hall) to which this once led, should enough funds be raised for this project sometime in the future. At the moment there are no such plans, but the long-term option remains.

Gigantentreppe, 1920 | Giant Staircase

Portal VI im Schlüterhof, Standort des künftigen Lapidariums | Portal VI in the Schlüter Courtyard, site of the lapidarium

Entwurf zur Bebauung der ehemaligen Altstadt auf historischem Grundriss, Bernd Albers, 2014 | Design for rebuilding the "old town" according to its historical layout

Korrespondenz zwischen Stellas Ostflügel und einer möglichen zeitgenössischen Bebauung des Marx-Engels-Forums. Bernd Albers, Altstadt Berlin, 2009 | Correspondence between Stella's east wing and possible contemporary buildings on the Marx-Engels-Forum

Von Osten gesehen, vom derzeitigen Marx-Engels-Forum aus, zeigt sich Stellas Architektur als adäquates Gegenüber des dort vorhandenen Stadtraums der Moderne. Seine Wasserseite leitet zu diesem über und schließt auch diesen in sich stimmig ab. Gleichzeitig eröffnet die Ostfassade aber auch die Möglichkeit, sollte es dereinst zu einer Nachverdichtung jenseits der Spree in zeitgenössischer Architektursprache kommen, auch mit dieser zu korrespondieren und eine Anbindung über die Spree hinweg zu ermöglichen.

Looking at the building from the east, from what is now the Marx-Engels-Forum, Stella's architecture presents itself as a suitable counterpart to the modern urban space on the other side of the river. His design for the waterfront façade forms a transition between the different urban spaces and provides a harmonious overall impression. At the same time, if the other side of the Spree should ever be built up with further contemporary buildings in the future, the east façade provides the possibility of correspondence with the new architecture and the creation of a connection across the river.

Stellas Wasserseite als Abschluss des Stadtraums der Moderne östlich der Spree | Stella's waterfront façade as a transition to the modern architecture

Die Westseite des Schlüter-hofs wie auch die Wassersei-te – hier befanden sich einst Architekturrudimente aus dem Mittelalter und der Re-naissance – präsentiert Stella in einer schlichten, sehr stren-gen Ausgestaltung. In ihrer Grammatik orientieren sich seine Fassadenachsen am barocken Raster. So nehmen diese die Geschosshöhen des Barockbaus auf, was das Gebäude enger verzahnt und Wege verkürzt. Die Fens-terflächen werden, stehend und mit Sprossen versehen, lediglich insoweit aufgewei-tet, dass der zusätzlich entste-hende Glasanteil die Bereiche kompensiert, die der barocke Schmuck ausmachen würde. Als Fassadenmaterial wählt Stella hierfür einen Architek-turbeton, dessen Oberfläche der des Sandsteins der re-konstruierten Fassaden äh-nelt, aber nicht gänzlich ent-spricht.

Stella schafft damit die Quad-ratur des Kreises. Seine hinzu-komponierten Gebäudeteile sind klar als Neuschöpfungen erkennbar, bauen sie aber gleichzeitig den barocken Bau auf logische, konsequen-te und völlig unaufgeregte Weise fort. Hatten viele Wett-bewerbskonkurrenten Extra-vaganzen aus Glas und Stahl vorgeschlagen, die das Ge-samtgebäude regelrecht als Karikatur erscheinen ließen, nimmt Stella sich bescheiden hinter dem Bestand zurück. Gleichzeitig unterscheiden sich seine Entwürfe genug vom Barockbau, so dass nie Gefahr besteht, dass Rekon-struktion und Neuschöpfung optisch verwischen.

Der rekonstruierte Schlüterhof gegenüber dem modernen Zwischentrakt |
Reconstructed Schlüter Courtyard bordered by the modern wing

Gegenüberstellung der Schlüter- und Stella-Achsen |
Comparison of axes by Schlüter and Stella

Wasserseite um 1939 | Waterfront façade around 1939

Stella's design of the west side of the Schlüter Courtyard and the waterfront façade – where remnants of medieval and renaissance architecture were formerly to be found – is characterised by simplicity and austerity. His façade axes essentially follow the baroque grid. The height of the floors is the same as those of the baroque building, giving the building a more compact appearance and shortening distances. The window areas, in upright orientation and with glazing bars, are only widened enough for the additional glass areas to compensate for the surfaces which would otherwise be occupied by baroque ornaments. Stella has chosen architectural concrete as material for these two façades; this is similar to but does not totally match the sandstone of the reconstructed façades.

In this way, Stella succeeds in merging two seemingly opposing concepts. The building components added by him are clearly identifiable as being new creations, but at the same time they prolong the baroque building's concept in a logical, consistent and totally unagitated manner. Whereas many of his competitors presented plans that included extravagant glass and steel features which made the overall building look like a caricature of itself, Stella's design takes a humble step back in favour of the former buildings. At the same time, his design is distinct enough from the original baroque building to avoid any visual blurring of the differences between the reconstructed and the newly-designed sections.

Barocke Neuschöpfung der Wasserseite, Entwurf von Sergei Tchoban | New baroque creation of the waterfront façade, design by Sergei Tchoban

Weitere Teilnehmer – Eine Auswahl

Die Liste der Wettbewerbsteilnehmer glich einem Who-is-who der Architekturszene des In- und Auslands. Sergei Tchoban, renommierter Architekt des Radisson-Komplexes nur unweit der Schlossbaustelle, hatte vorgeschlagen, das zu verwirklichen, was man früher nie vermocht hatte. Ihm schwebte vor, an der Wasserseite eine barocke Seite „hinzuzuerfinden", die es historisch nie gegeben hat – was aber erstmals nach allen Seiten ein einheitliches Gebäude suggeriert hätte. Im abschließenden Juryentscheid setzte er sich damit nicht durch.

Hans Kollhoff, Drittplatzierter im Wettbewerb, offerierte ebenfalls eine ästhetisch ansprechende Variante. Nur verlegte er wichtige Verbindungsgänge wenig attraktiv ins Untergeschoss und projektierte einen Empfangsbereich, der, einem Lichtspielhaus ähnelnd, sich schwerlich ins Gesamtkonzept einfügte.

Einen nachträglichen Sturm im Wasserglas verursachte Architekt Stefan Braunfels, der mit seinem Beitrag im Wettbewerb ebenfalls unterlag. In einer sich über Monate hinziehenden Medienkampagne versuchte er noch nach Baubeginn Sympathien für sein äußerlich ebenfalls gänzlich

barockes, zum Fluss hin geöffnetes Schloss zu wecken. Dass der Schlüterhof, einmal zur Spree hin um einen Flügel verkürzt, als Konzertort akustisch unbrauchbar wäre, die Wegeführung im Bauwerk dramatisch eingeschränkt, ein umgedrehter Schlüterhof – denn den schlug er tatsächlich vor – eine spätere Rekonstruktion der Innenräume unmöglich machen würde, schien für ihn nicht zu zählen. Seine Vorschläge wurden nicht zur Kenntnis genommen. Der Bau schritt fort und blieb im Zeit- und Kostenrahmen, insbesondere auch, weil Planänderungen während der Bauphase von vornherein ausgeschlossen worden waren.

Das zur Spree hin geöffnete Schloss von Stefan Braunfels | Design by Stefan Braunfels with the palace opening out onto the Spree

Der Schlüterhof mit historisierender Westfassade von Hans Kollhoff | Schlüter courtyard and a west façade with historical look, by Hans Kollhoff

Some of the other competitors

The list of participants in the competition reads like a who's who of the German and international architecture world. Sergei Tchoban, a renowned architect who designed the Radisson Complex in the immediate vicinity of the palace site, suggested something that history had failed to achieve. His idea was to "invent" an additional baroque façade, which had actually never existed, on the waterfront side. This would have presented the palace as a homogeneous building in all directions for the first time in history. His concept did not convince the jury, however. Hans Kollhoff, who was awarded third place, also proposed an aesthetically pleasing concept. However, the fact that he located important passageways in the basement was less attractive and the lobby design looked very much like a cinema, which did not really fit into the overall concept.

Empfangshalle von Hans Kollhoff | Entrance lobby by Hans Kollhoff

Architect Stefan Braunfels, whose contribution did not convince the jury either, managed to create a storm in a teacup long after the competition had been concluded. He kicked off a media campaign lasting for several months, even after construction work had already started, to find supporters for his design of an entirely baroque palace opening out onto the river. It did not seem important to him that removing a wing of the Schlüter Courtyard would make it completely unsuitable as a con-cert venue from the acoustics aspect and would drastically limit routing options within the building, and that turning the courtyard around by 180 degrees – something which he actually suggested – would make any later reconstruction of the palace rooms impossible. His suggestions were ignored. The construction work was continued on-time and on-budget, in particular due to the fact that making changes to the plans during ongoing construction had been ruled out right from the start.

Bernd Albers konzipierte auf der Ostseite ein Hochhaus. Der so genannte „Humboldt-Tower" wäre als Landmarke von fernher sichtbar gewesen.

Einen vornehm-klassischen, für die Jury vielleicht zu klassischen Vorschlag lieferte das Büro Nöfer, das eine zusätzliche Brücke über die Spree vorsah, mittels derer man das Gebäude von Osten aus hätte begehen können.

Von der Problematik, die geforderte Rekonstruktion mit einer eigenen, prägnanten Handschrift zu verschmelzen, zeugen dagegen die Entwürfe anderer Büros. f-s-Architekten suchten keine Harmonie zwischen Alt und Neu, sie setzten klar auf Brüche. Auch Busmann + Haberer planten, sich mit ausdrucksstarken Gegensätzen das Schloss Untertan zu machen.

Bernd Albers's concept envisaged a high-rise building on the east side. This so-called "Humboldt Tower" would have been a landmark visible from afar.

The architect's office Nöfer presented an elegant and classical concept, maybe a bit too classical for the jury. It included an additional bridge over the Spree, making the building accessible from the east.

The designs of various other architects show how difficult it was to merge the stipulated reconstruction features with their own individual style. f-s-Architekten made no attempt to seek harmony between old and new, they focused quite clearly on a break in style. Busmann + Haberer also planned to dominate the palace by vivid contrasts.

Der „Humboldt-Tower" von Bernd Albers vom Schlüterhof aus gesehen |
The "Humboldt Tower" envisaged by Bernd Albers, seen from the Schlüter Courtyard

Ein Querriegel an der Spree, fast so groß wie das Schloss selber, dominiert über den Barockbau (Busmann + Haberer) |

Das von Osten über eine neue Brücke zu erreichende Schloss des Büro Nöfer | Design by Nöfer: the palace is accessed from the east over a new bridge

f-s Architekten setzen auf ein Spannungsverhältnis zwischen rekonstruierter Fassade und zeitgenössischer Ausgestaltung | f-s Architekten relies on a strong contrast between the reconstructed façade and contemporary design

A crosswing along the Spree, almost as big as the actual palace, dominates the baroque building (Busmann + Haberer)

Die Bildhauer von heute

Etwa dreihundert Fragmente der Schlossfassade haben die Zeit überdauert. War im August 1950 seitens der DDR-Regierung die Schlosssprengung verkündet worden, ist es Gegnern des Abrisses zuvor in Eigenregie gelungen, wichtigste Skulpturen aus der Ruine zu bergen. Doch aus Überbleibseln alleine lässt sich das Schloss nicht rekonstruieren, auch lassen sich diese kaum mehr der Witterung aussetzen. Der Großteil musste basierend auf Fotografien und Bauzeichnungen neu geschaffen werden.

Der Bildhauer der Gegenwart operiert dabei wie sein Pendant vor dreihundert Jahren. In Ton modelliert er das entsprechende Stück – zunächst als Miniatur, als so genanntes *bozzetto*, dann erneut in der originalen Größe, bis es von einer hochrangigen Expertenkommission abgenommen wird. Eine Gipsabformung dient dann als Vorlage für den Steinbildhauer, das jeweilige Schmuckelement im Punktierverfahren in Sandstein zu übertragen. Zum Einsatz kommt hierbei sächsischer wie auch schlesischer Sandstein. In der Schlossbauhütte in Berlin-Spandau arbeitet ein Bildhauerteam seit Jahren mit Hochdruck an der Erschaffung der Modelle. An der Umsetzung in Stein sind Betriebe bundesweit beteiligt und setzen dabei auch modernste Frästechnik ein. Doch werden auch im maschinellen Verfahren lediglich Rohlinge gefertigt. Die letzten Zentimeter, dort wo sich die Handwerkskunst des Einzelnen zeigt, entstehen nach wie vor per Hand.

The sculptors of today

Around three hundred fragments of the palace façade have survived. After the East German government announced its decision to demolish the palace in August 1950, opponents managed to rescue major sculptures from the palace ruins. It is impossible, however, to reconstruct the palace merely on the basis of these remnants and it would not be advisable to expose the fragments to the elements, either. This meant that most of the façade had to be rebuilt on the basis of photographs and architectural drawings.

Present-day sculptors use the same methods as their colleagues did three hundred years ago. The sculptor creates a clay model of the object – first only a small scale model, the so-called *bozzetto*, and then a full-sized model which is presented to a high-level expert committee for approval. A plaster cast serves as a template for the stone carver, who copies the ornament to the sandstone with the aid of a pointing machine. Saxon and Silesian sandstone is used for this purpose. For several years now, a team of sculptors has been pressing ahead with creating the models at the "palace building lodge" (Schlossbauhütte) in Berlin-Spandau. Companies from all over Germany are involved in carving the models in stone, some of them using the latest milling technology. But in the end, the machines can only create rough copies. The final touches, the steps which require individual craftsmanship, are still done by hand.

Abrissgegner bergen wichtige Skulpturen, 1950 | Important sculptures are rescued

Die geretteten Kolossalfiguren des Schlüterhofs | Collossal statues from the Schlüter Courtyard were rescued

Beim Modellieren eines Festons | Modelling a festoon

Die Anschlusskartusche der Eosanderschulter als Gipsmodell | Plaster model of cartouche

Übertragung eines Adlers in Stein | Carving an eagle in stone

Modellierarbeiten | Modelling details by hand

Eine moderne Fräse im Einsatz | Modern milling machines are used

Die fertige Anschlusskartusche in Stein | The finished stone cartouche

Die Bautechnik

Während der Hochbauphase ragte lange Zeit ein riesiger Betonklotz aus der Mitte Berlins. Dies brachte dem Projekt Spottnamen wie „das Vorhängeschloss" ein. Nichts liegt der Wahrheit ferner. Zwar gewährleistet das innere Betontragwerk in Kombination mit einer Dämmschicht ein zeitgemäßes Niedrigenergiehaus, doch ist es eine gänzlich unabhängige, sich selbst tragende Ziegelkonstruktion von fünfundsechzig Zentimetern Stärke, die die Sandsteinelemente, wie schon in früheren Zeiten, statisch fasst. Beim Schloss handelt sich um das größte Ziegelbauwerk der Nachkriegsgeschichte, werden doch hier mehr als dreieinhalb Millionen Ziegel verbaut. Somit vereint das Vorhaben heutige Nutzungsansprüche mit akribischer Wiederherstellung des Alten.

Building techniques

For a long time during aboveground construction work, Berlin's centre was dominated by a huge concrete block. A lot of people joked that the façade was just going to be "hung" over this, but nothing could be further from the truth. Although the inner concrete shell, in combination with an insulating layer, ensures that the building complies with modern low-energy requirements, the sandstone elements are borne by an independent, sixty-five centimetres thick self-supporting brick structure. The palace is the largest brick building to be built in post-war history, consisting of more than three and a half million bricks. Thus the project unites modern functional requirements with a meticulous reconstruction of the old structure.

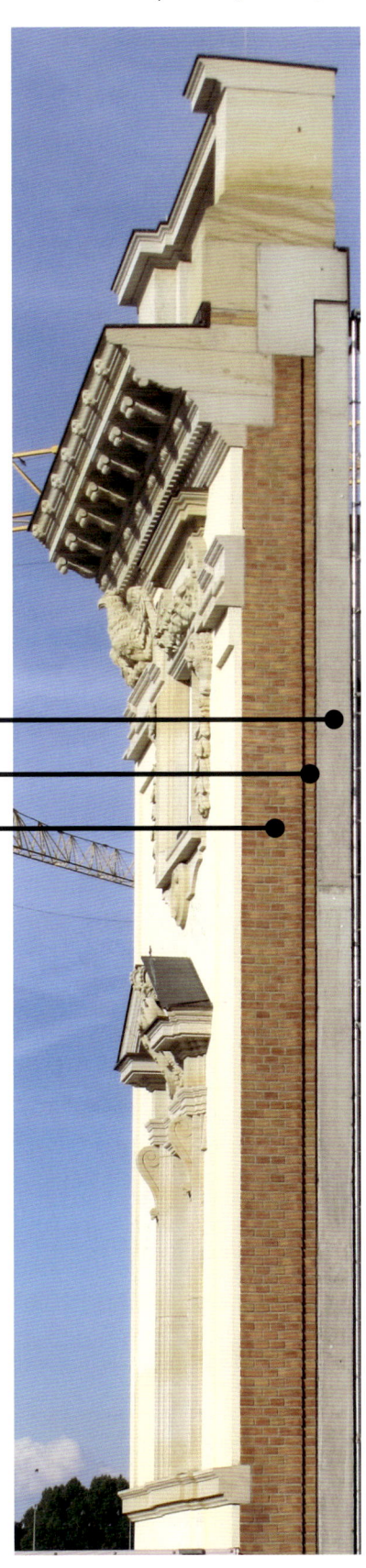

Betonkern | Concrete core (30 cm)

Dämmung | Insulation (10 cm)

Ziegelmauerwerk | Brickwork (65 cm)

Der Verein

Ohne Initiator Wilhelm von Boddien gäbe es kein Schloss. Zusammen mit dem von ihm gegründeten Verein und vielen engagierten Ehrenamtlichen ebnete er den Weg für die Wiederherstellung des Gebäudes, in das er sich nach eigener Aussage einst verliebt hatte, ohne es je selbst gesehen zu haben. Seit Jahren trägt sein Verein die Begeisterung für dieses Vorhaben in die Bevölkerung. Allein in den Jahren 2014 und 2015 konnten so Spenden in Höhe von jeweils 15 Millionen gesammelt werden. Anfang 2018 waren 79 Millionen beisammen. Das Schloss ist auf einem sehr guten Wege, doch noch ist die Schlacht nicht geschlagen. Jede noch so kleine Spende hilft!

The "Association Berliner Schloss"

If it were not for Wilhelm von Boddien, the originator of the idea, there would be no palace. He and the association he founded, together with many dedicated volunteers, prepared the ground for reconstruction of the building, which he claims to have fallen in love with without ever having seen it. His association has been conveying this enthusiasm for the project to the general public for many years now. In 2014 and 2015 alone, they managed to raise donations of 15 million euros per year. By the beginning of 2018, the sum of 79 million euros had been collected. The palace is well on its way to completion, but the final battle has not yet been won. Every donation, however small, helps.

Ehrenamtliche erläutern städtebauliche Zusammenhänge an Horst Dührings Modell |
Volunteers explain the urban context using Horst Dühring's historical model

Ehrenamtliche befreien die Schlossfundamente von Unkraut und halten das Schloss in den Köpfen präsent |
Volunteers remove weeds from the palace foundation and keep memories of the palace alive

Im Sommer 2011 ist noch nicht zu erahnen, dass hinter der Humboldt-Box ein Schloss wiederentsteht, das sie schon bald überragen wird | In summer 2011, it is still difficult to imagine that behind the Humboldt-Box a palace is being reborn and will soon tower over it

Wilhelm von Boddien führt durch die Berliner Bildhauerwerkstätten | Wilhelm von Boddien showing visitors around the sculptors' studios

Die Humboldt-Box

Seit 2011 ist der Förderverein in der Humboldt-Box vertreten – einer Informationsplattform am Ort des Geschehens, ausgestaltet in einer expressiven Architektursprache, die Zweiflern vor Augen führt, wie sehr ein restlos modern konzipiertes Gebäude den historischen Gebäudekontext gestört hätte. Der temporäre Bau bietet ein Fenster in das spannende Geschehen auf der Schlossbaustelle. Herzstück der Ausstellung ist das Stadtmodell des Kunstlehrers Horst Dühring – eine faszinierende Darstellung der Berliner Mitte um 1900, die mehr als fünfzehn Jahre Arbeit einforderte.

The Humboldt Box

The association has had its own exhibition in the Humboldt Box since 2011. This is an on-site information platform, designed in an expressive architectural style that clearly demonstrates – in case anyone is still in doubt – how a totally modern construction would have upset the historical building context. This temporary structure provides a window to the exciting events happening on the palace construction site. The exhibition showpiece, a model of the city that took arts teacher, Horst Dühring, more than 15 years to complete, gives visitors a fascinating impression of Berlin's city centre around 1900.

Navigationsobjekte aus Ozeanien im speziell dafür konzipierten, zwei Etagen einnehmenden Ausstellungssaal | Oceanian navigation display in a specially designed, two-storey exhibition hall

Das Humboldt-Forum

Ein Ort der Weltkulturen, ein Haus der Völkerverständigung wird 2019 im Herzen Berlins eröffnen. Das erste Stockwerk nimmt den Besucher mit einer Berlin-Ausstellung in Empfang, die die Hauptstadt im globalen Kontext – im Austausch mit der Welt und umgekehrt – porträtiert, den Bogen zu Wilhelm und Alexander von Humboldt spannt und sich als „Brücke" zwischen dem Standort Berlin und dem Eintauchen in die Kulturen Afrikas, Asiens, Ozeaniens und Amerikas versteht. Diese wird im Parade- und Mezzaningeschoss auf 20.000 Quadratmetern durch Exponate der ethnologischen Sammlungen der Staatlichen Museen zu Berlin repräsentiert: afrikanische Masken, chinesisches Porzellan, Mumien und Schriftzeugnisse indigener Völker Amerikas, Navigationsobjekte aus Ozeanien. Die bislang in Berlin-Dahlem beheimatete völkerkundliche Sammlung kehrt damit ins Schloss zurück – handelt es sich doch dabei um einen Ort, der ihr alles andere als fremd ist, liegen ihre Ursprünge hier.

Doch auch wenn bereits der Große Kurfürst Friedrich Wilhelm von Brandenburg ein besonderes Interesse für Kunst aus Asien, Afrika und Brasilien hegte, er und seine Nachfolger sich Verdienste als Sammler erwarben, kehren die Kunstkammern nun allenfalls als Paraphrase wieder. Anders als in der wissenschaftlich unbegleiteten Schau der Hohenzollern ist der Anspruch heute ein gänzlich anderer. Der multiperspektivische Blick auf die jeweiligen Objektgeschichten ist zentral, so bleibt nicht unkommentiert, unter welchen Umständen bestimmte Objekte ihre Reise nach Berlin antraten. Koloniale Schuld soll keine Tabuisierung erfahren, moralische Implikationen treten in den Blickpunkt. Der Umgang mit den Exponaten erfolgt dabei in enger Kooperation mit den jeweiligen nationalen Instituten vor Ort.

Innenarchitektur des Büro Applebaum |
Interior architecture by Applebaum

Westafrika-Bereich (Benin) | West Africa section (Benin)

Maske der Torres-Strait-Inseln, 1860 |
Mask from the Torres Strait Islands

Garderobe | Cloakroom

The Humboldt Forum

A home for the cultures of the world, a house of international understanding is due to open in the heart of Berlin in 2019. Visitors will be greeted on the first floor by an exhibition portraying Berlin in a global context and its interaction with the world at large. This exhibition will also show the links to Wilhelm and Alexander von Humboldt and create a "bridge" between Berlin and the cultures of Africa, Asia, Oceania and America. Visitors can immerse themselves in these cultures, which will be presented on 20,000 square metres of the parade and mezzanine floor in the form of exhibits from ethnological collections of the Berlin National Museums (Staatliche Museen zu Berlin): masks from Africa, porcelain from China, mummies and written records of indigenous people from America and navigation aids from Oceania, to name but a few. The ethnological collection, currently housed in Berlin-Dahlem, will finally be returning to the Berlin Palace – which is where the collection has its roots.

Even though the Great Elector, Frederick William of Brandenburg, was particularly interested in art from Asia, Africa and Brazil, and he and his successors earned much acclaim as collectors, the former art chambers will be returning at the most as a paraphrase. In contrast to the exhibitions staged by the Hohenzollern dynasty, which had the sole aim of "displaying" the exhibits and lacked any kind of scientific accompaniment, modern museums have totally different aspirations. One of the central aims is to take a multiple-perspective look at the history of individual objects, including discussions about the conditions under which the objects were brought to Berlin. This also means addressing the issue of colonial guilt, and bringing moral implications into focus. To achieve this aim, exhibitions will be staged in close cooperation with the relevant national institutions of the countries of origin.

Nach Vorbild der namensgebenden Gebrüder von Humboldt wird auch der Aspekt der Lehre nicht außen vor bleiben. Das *Humboldt-Lab* gewährt Einblick in aktuelle Forschungsprojekte aller universitären Fachrichtungen mit konkretem Alltagsbezug. Sonderausstellungsbereiche im Erdgeschoss setzen sich mit aktuellen globalpolitischen Ereignissen auseinander und präsentieren zeitgenössische europäische und nicht-europäische Kulturen gemeinsam und auf Augenhöhe. Selbst das sogenannte *Restaurant der Kontinente* ist eng mit dem Gesamtkonzept verwoben und lädt dazu ein, afrikanische und asiatische Küche kulinarisch zu erfahren. Auch auf dem Dach, das einen spektakulären Blick über die Berliner Mitte ermöglicht, wird es Gastronomie geben.

Following the example of Wilhelm and Alexander von Humboldt, the brothers who gave the forum its name, the educational aspect will also play a major role. The *Humboldt-Lab* will give an insight into current research projects at all universities and their relevance to everyday life. Special exhibition areas on the ground floor will deal with current geopolitical events and will present contemporary European and non-European cultures on an equal level. Even the so-called *Restaurant der Kontinente* will follow the global concept and give visitors the opportunity to try African and Asian cuisine. There will be additional catering facilities on the rooftop, offering a spectacular view of Berlin's city centre.

Begehbares Archäologisches Fenster mit erhaltenen …

Schloss und Dachcafé | Palace with rooftop café

Im Untergeschoss beschäftigt sich der Bau dann mit sich selbst. Auf einer Fläche von 1800 Quadratmetern war es möglich, erhalten gebliebene Kellerräume des alten Schlosses in die Rekonstruktion zu integrieren. Dort sind jene Sprengkrater ersichtlich, wo im Zuge der Vernichtung des Gebäudes das Dynamit platziert worden war. In der ehemaligen Wachstube des Kommandanten und der alten Heizungsanlage können die Besucher künftig die in ihrer Wechselhaftigkeit beispiellose Geschichte dieses Ortes erfahren. Nicht zuletzt ein Modell der gläsernen Blume, die einst das Foyer des Palastes der Republik zierte, findet in diesem Museum wieder eine Heimstatt.

Meanwhile, in the basement, the building will occupy itself with its own history. Fortunately it was possible to integrate some of the Palace's remaining cellar spaces, covering an area of 1,800 square metres, into reconstruction of the building. Here visitors can see the craters left by the dynamite used for demolition. In the former commander's guardroom and the old heating cellars they can learn about the history of this site and its unparalleled diversity. And, last but not least, a model of the glass flower that used to adorn the foyer of the Palast der Republik has found a new home here.

... Kellerfragmenten des Schlosses | Archeological window with cellar fragments

Gläserne Blume im Palast der Republik, 1990 | Glass flower in the Palace of the Republic

Zeitgenössischer Querriegel Stellas mit dem zentralen Treppenhaus | Stella's contemporary cross-wing with the central staircase

Damit schließt das als Humboldt-Forum wiederaufgebaute Berliner Schloss architektonisch und städtebaulich die schmerzhafte Wunde, die 1950 hier entstanden war. Inhaltlich komplettiert das Humboldt-Forum die Museumsinsel und stellt die nichteuropäische Kultur der europäischen in gleichberechtigter Weise gegenüber. Architektonisch lässt der Bau das minutiös aufeinander abgestimmte historische Bauensemble der Berliner Mitte wieder aufleben und ermöglicht nach Osten hin außerdem eine Anbindung jener Stadtbereiche, die lange ein Schattendasein führten, nun aber wieder in den Fokus gerückt werden. Bürgerliches Engagement hat dieses Wunder möglich gemacht.

The reconstructed Berlin Palace, alias Humboldt Forum, will finally heal the wound in the architectural and urban structure of Berlin that was torn open in 1950. The Humboldt Forum will complement the Museumsinsel in terms of content by displaying non-European cultures on an equal footing with European culture. From the architectural aspect, the building will revive the historical ensemble that once harmonised so beautifully in the centre of the city. It will also form a link eastwards to those parts of the city which were neglected for so long, but are now returning to the focus of public attention. The tremendous commitment of citizens in Germany and other parts of the world has made this dream come true.

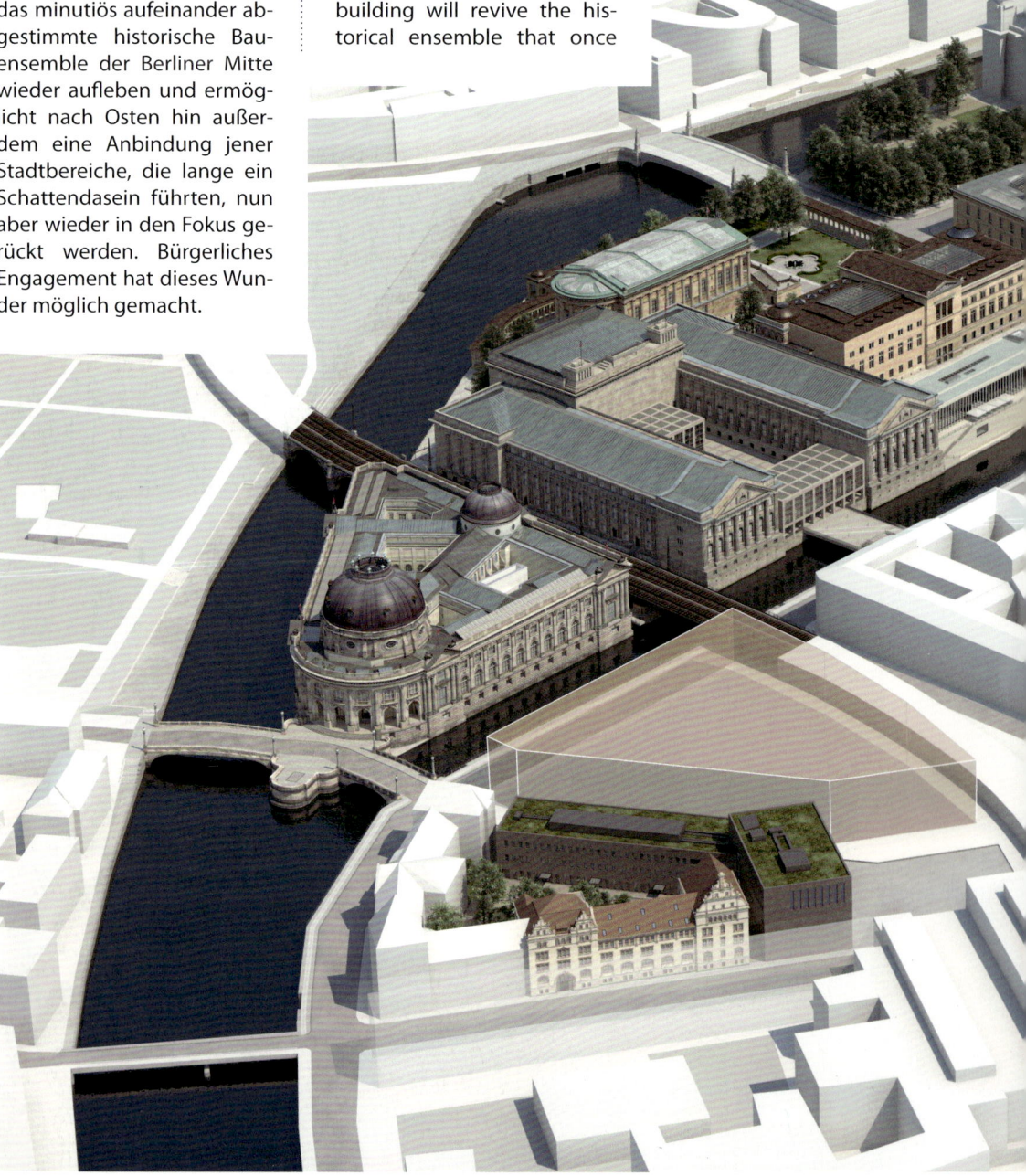

Simulation der zukünftigen Museumsinsel Berlin und des Humboldt-Forums, Blick von Nordwesten | Simulation of the future Museum Island and Humboldt Forum,